Did God really say,

You must not eat from any tree in the garden?

Genesis 3:1

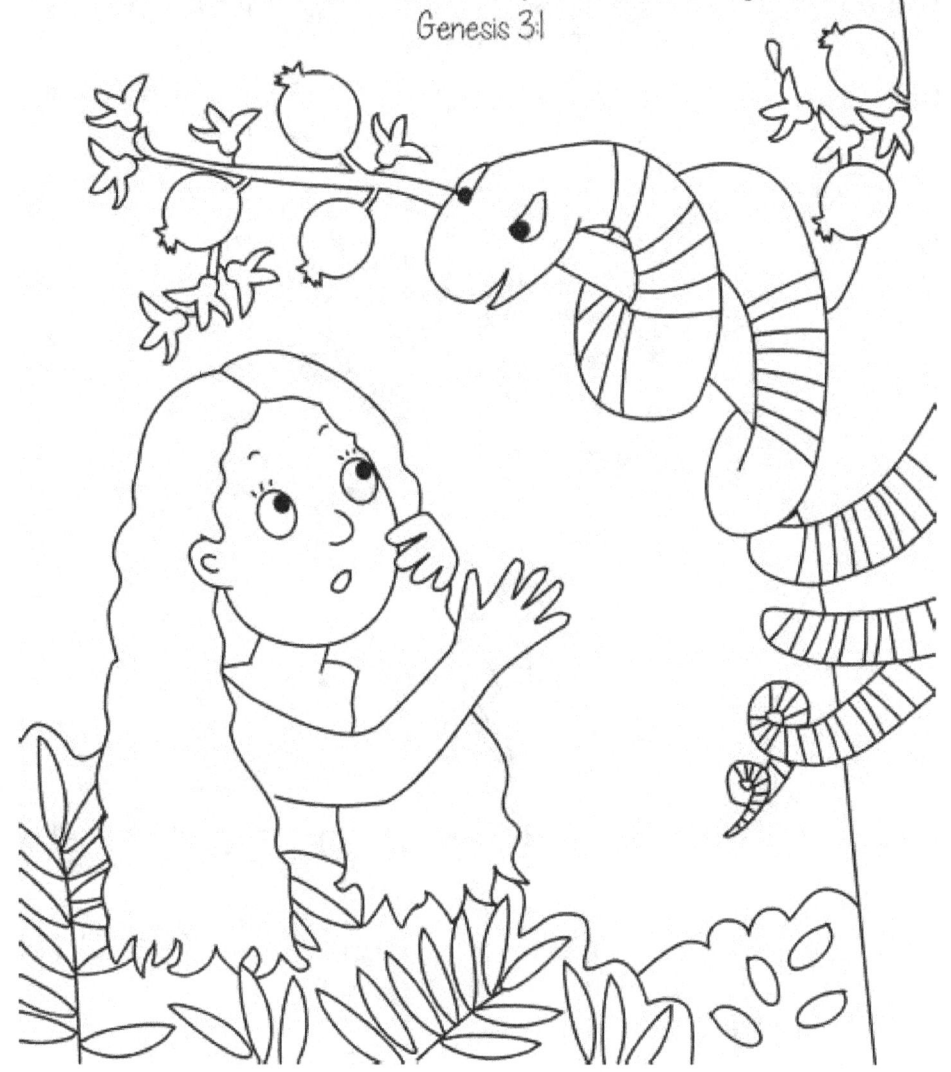

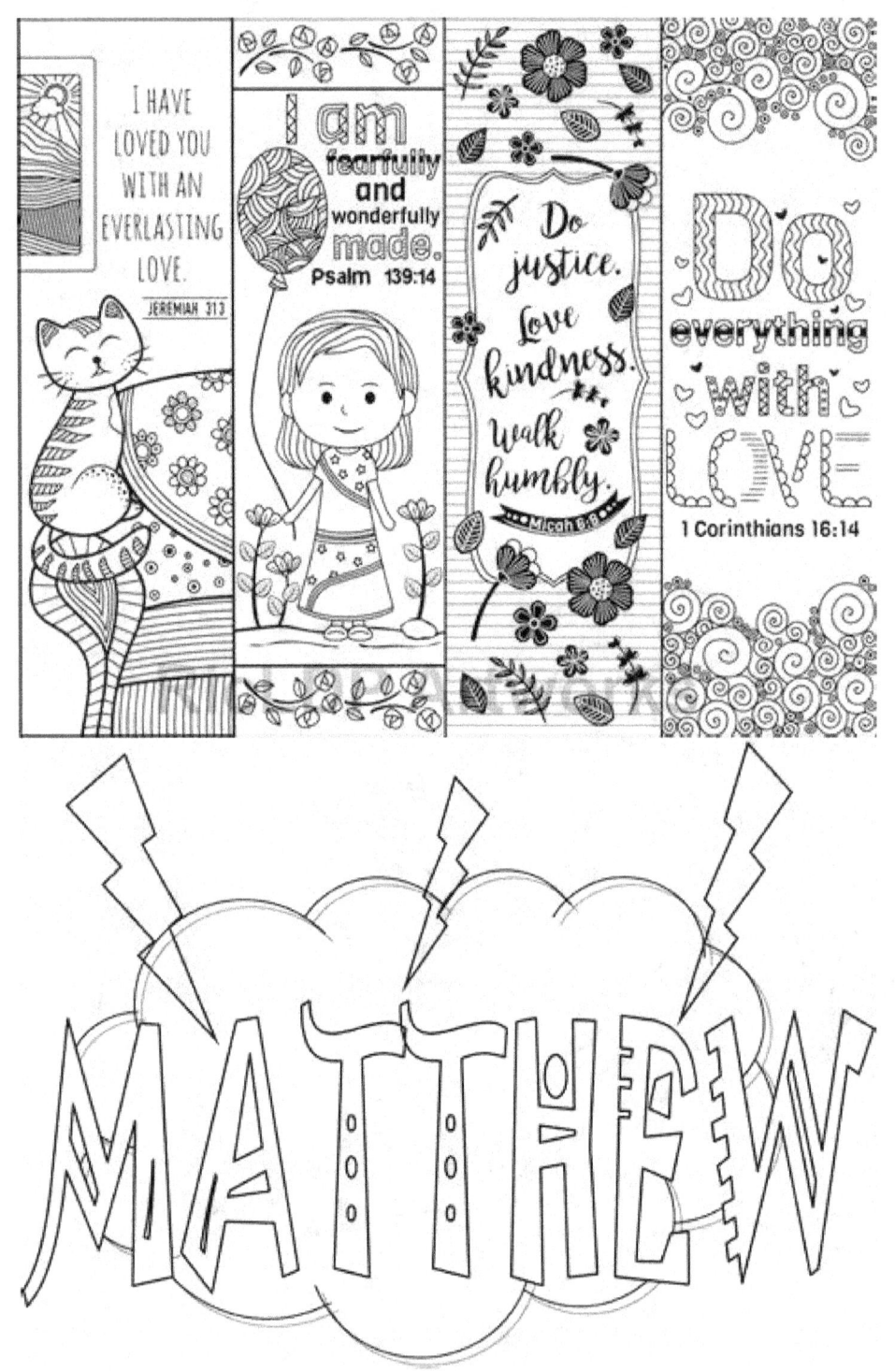

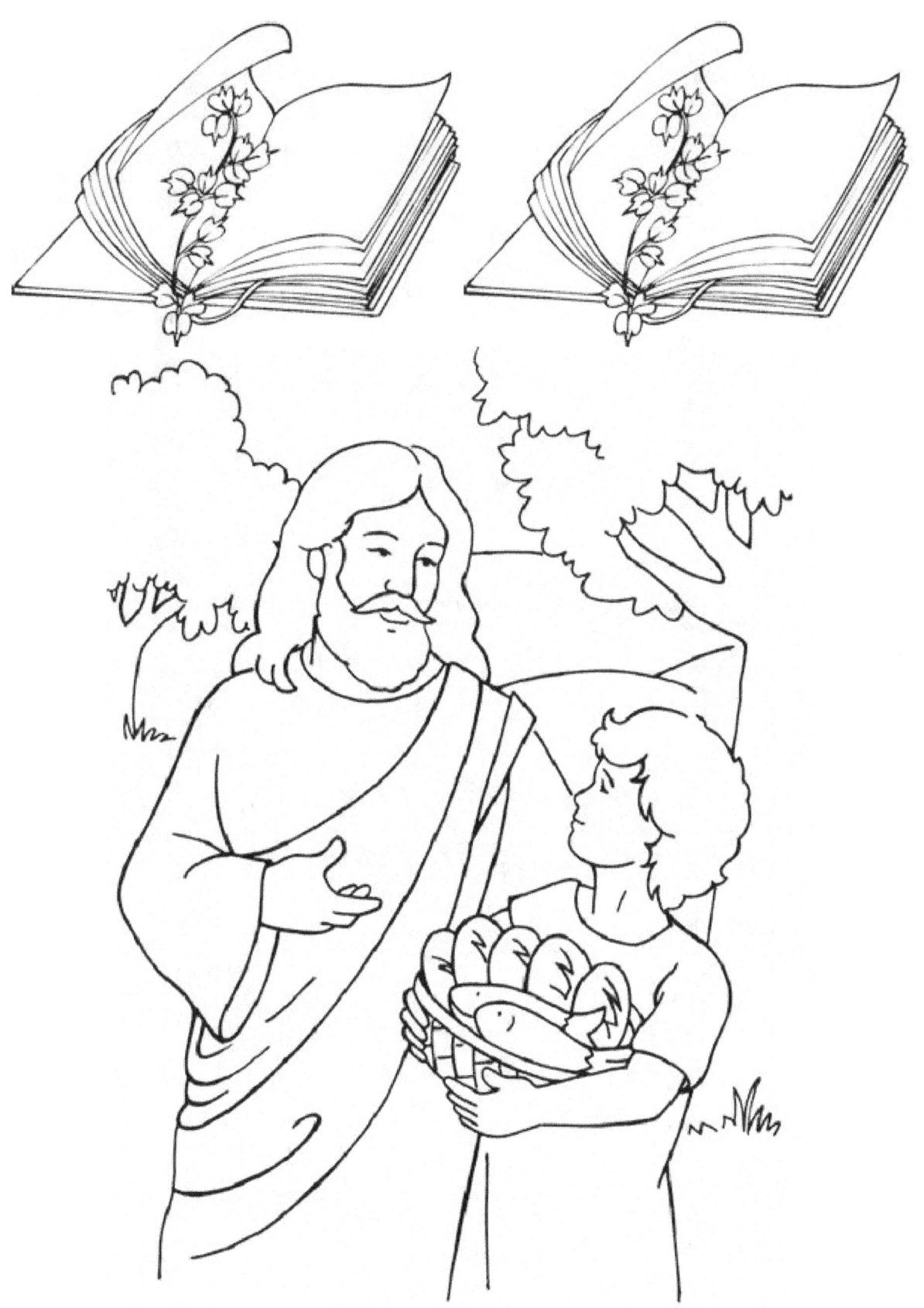

Bible Old Testament

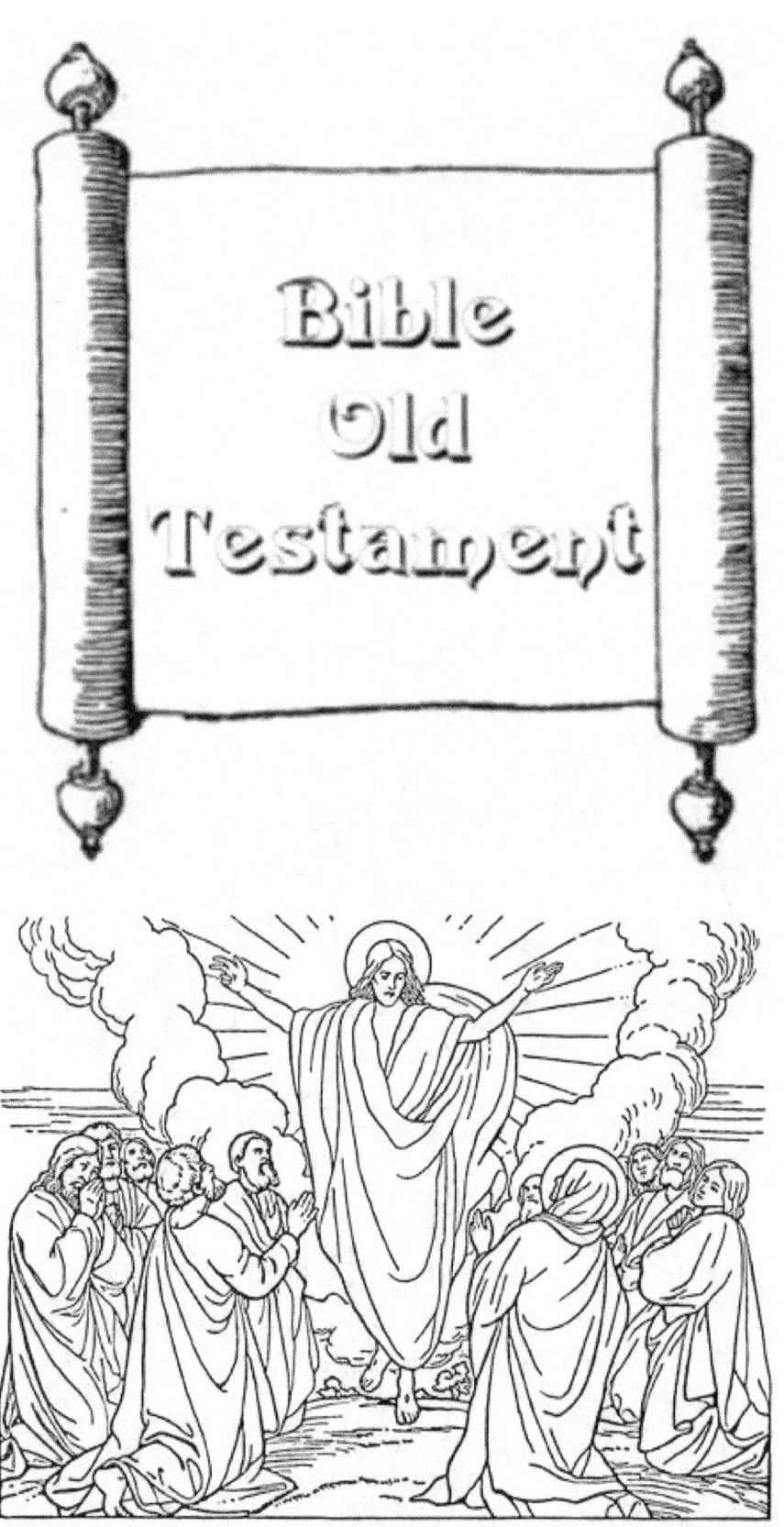

I John
4:7-12

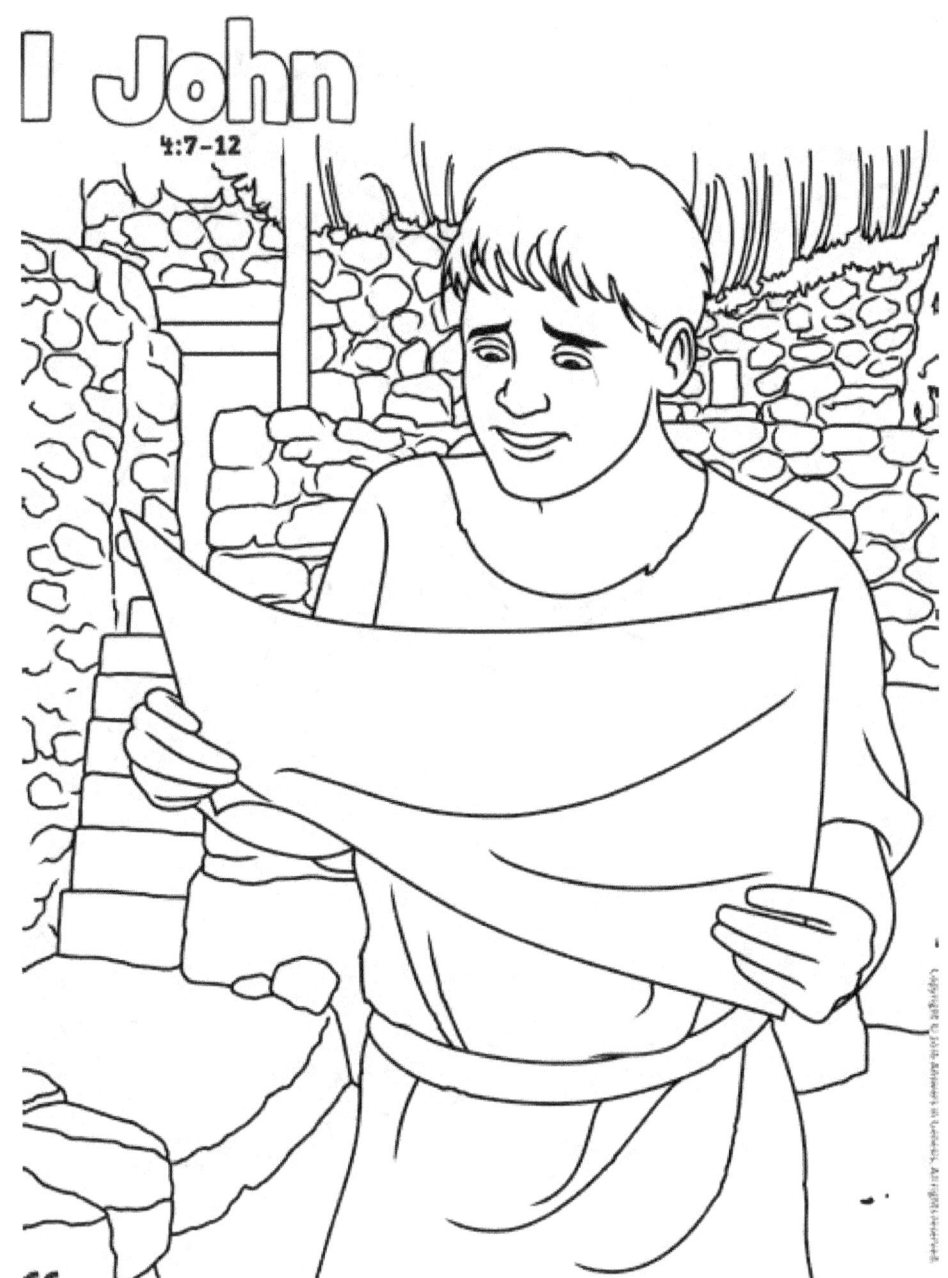

66

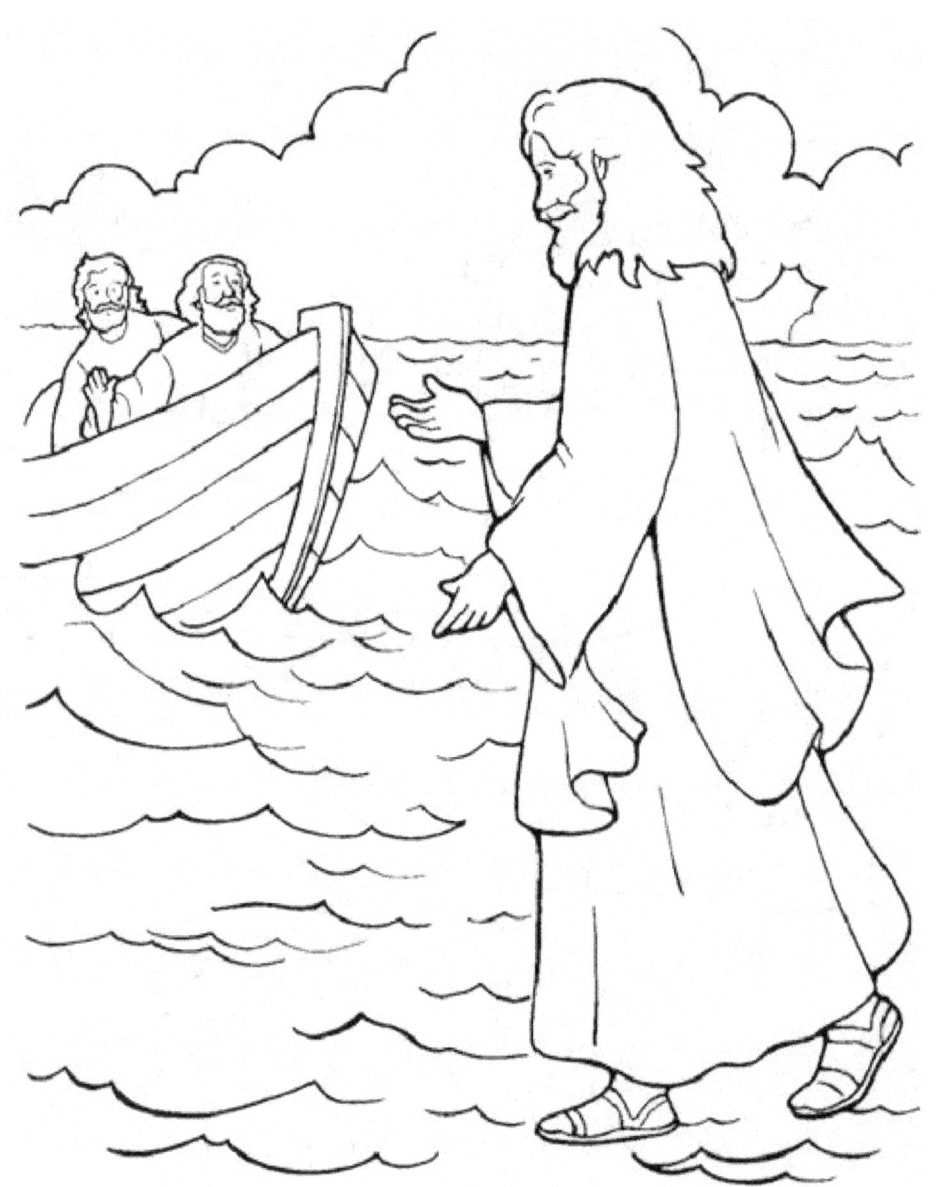

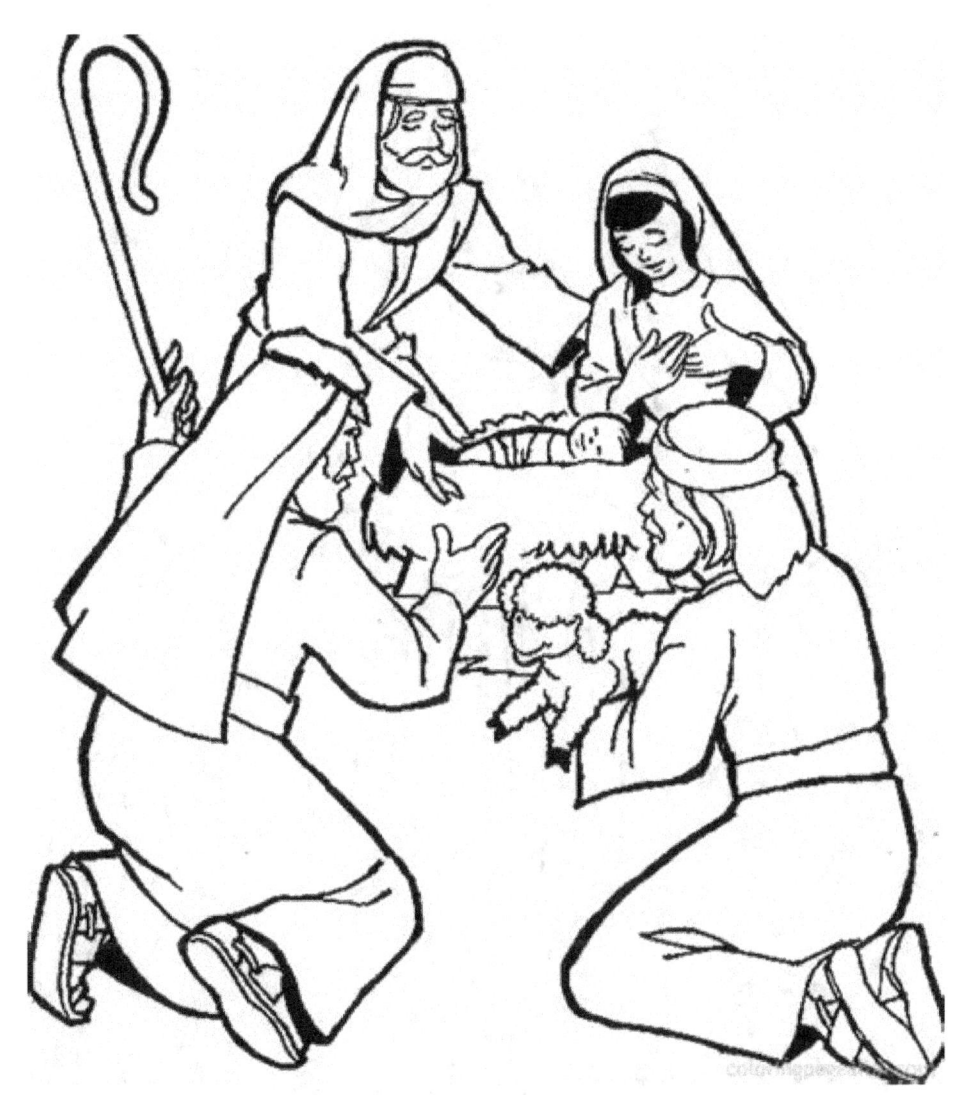

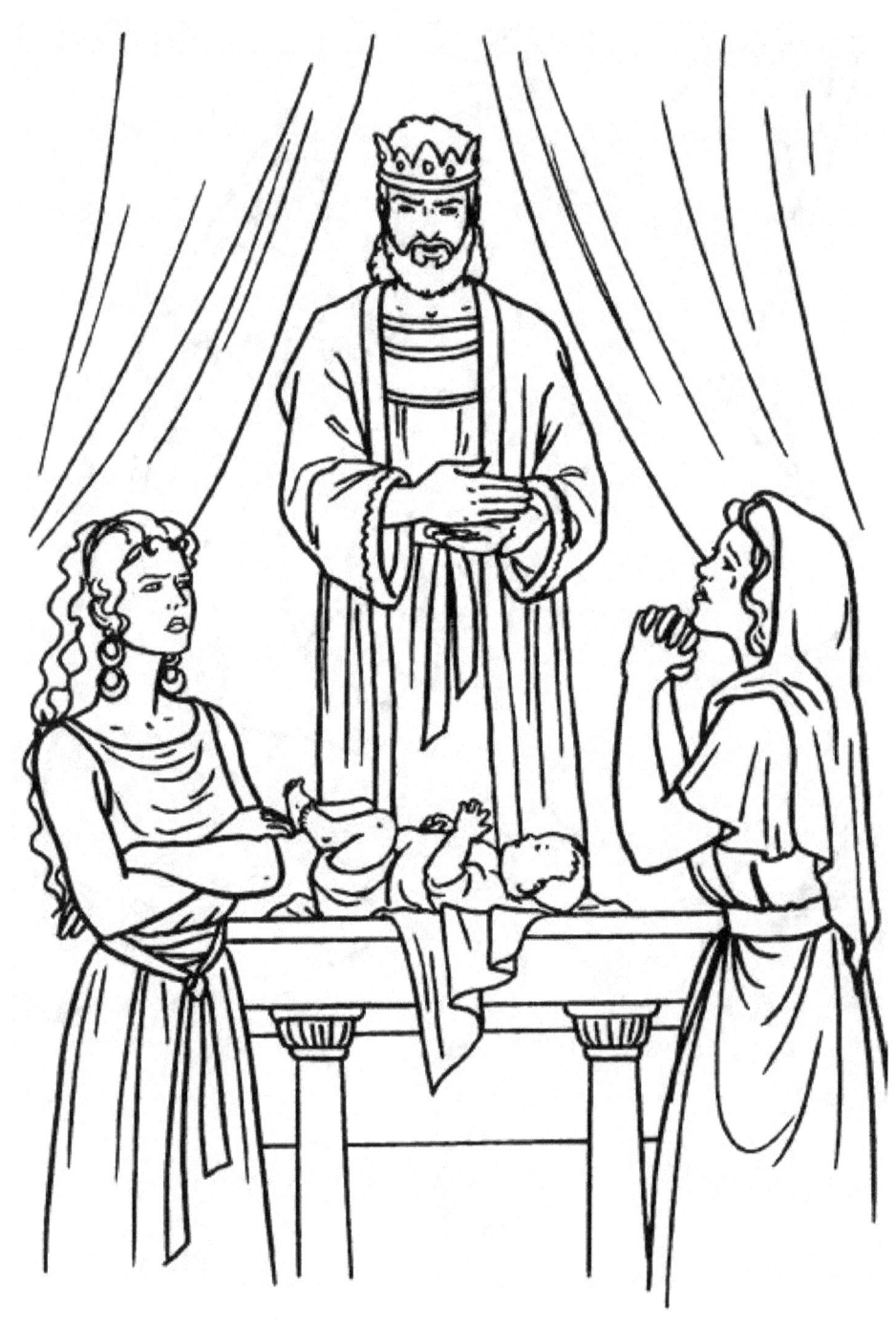

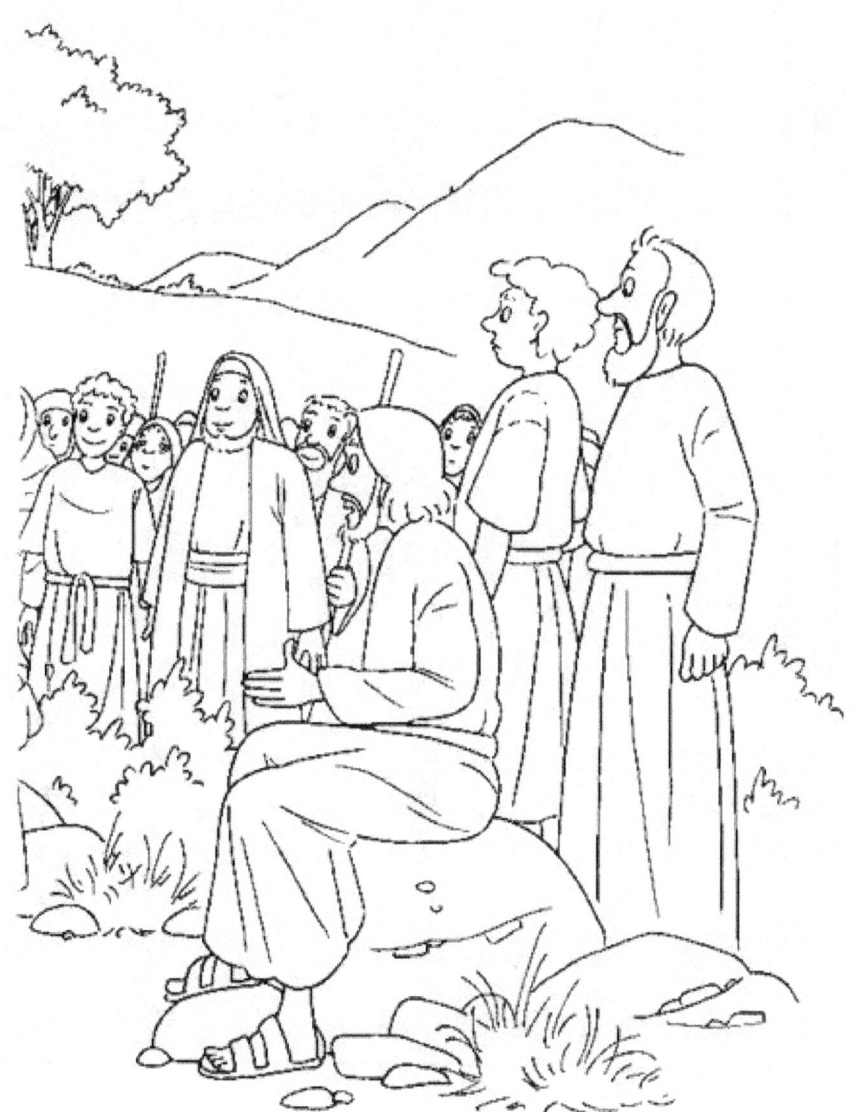

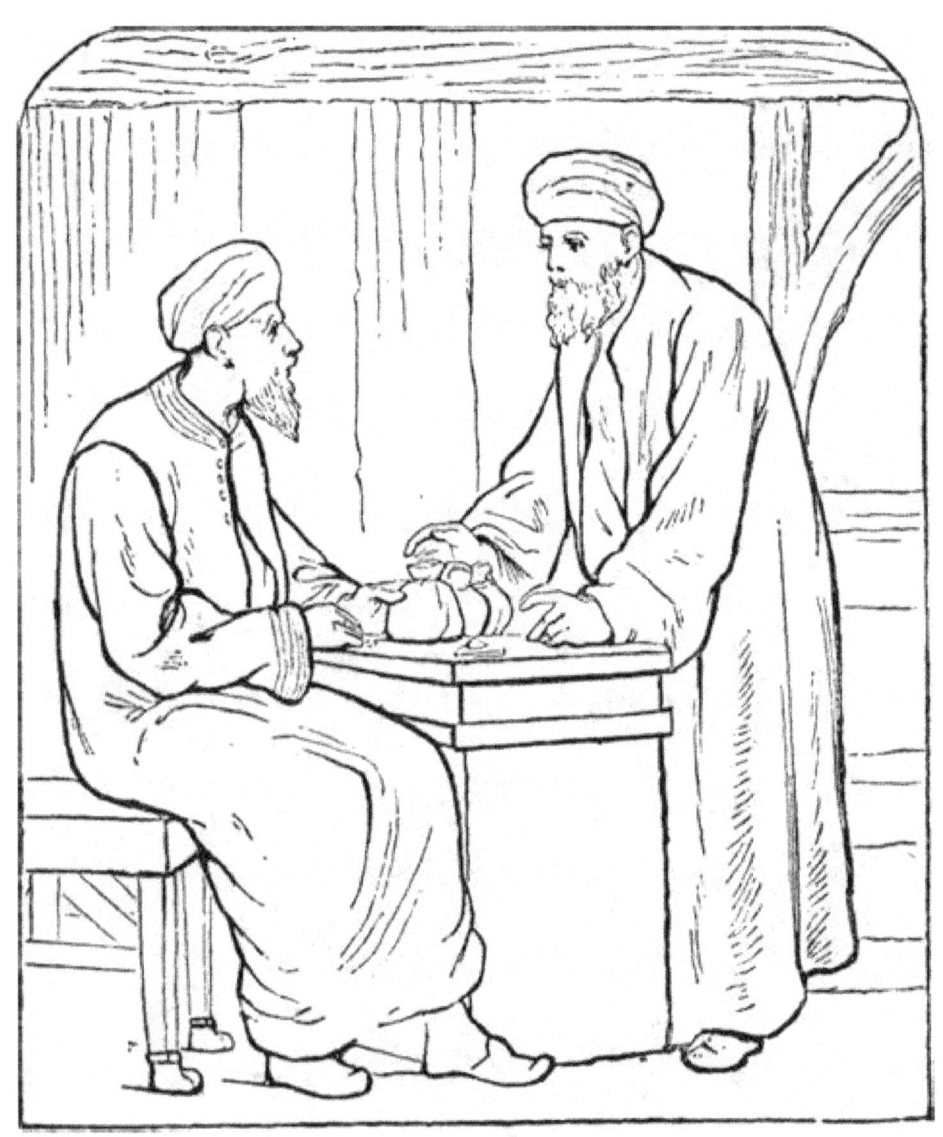

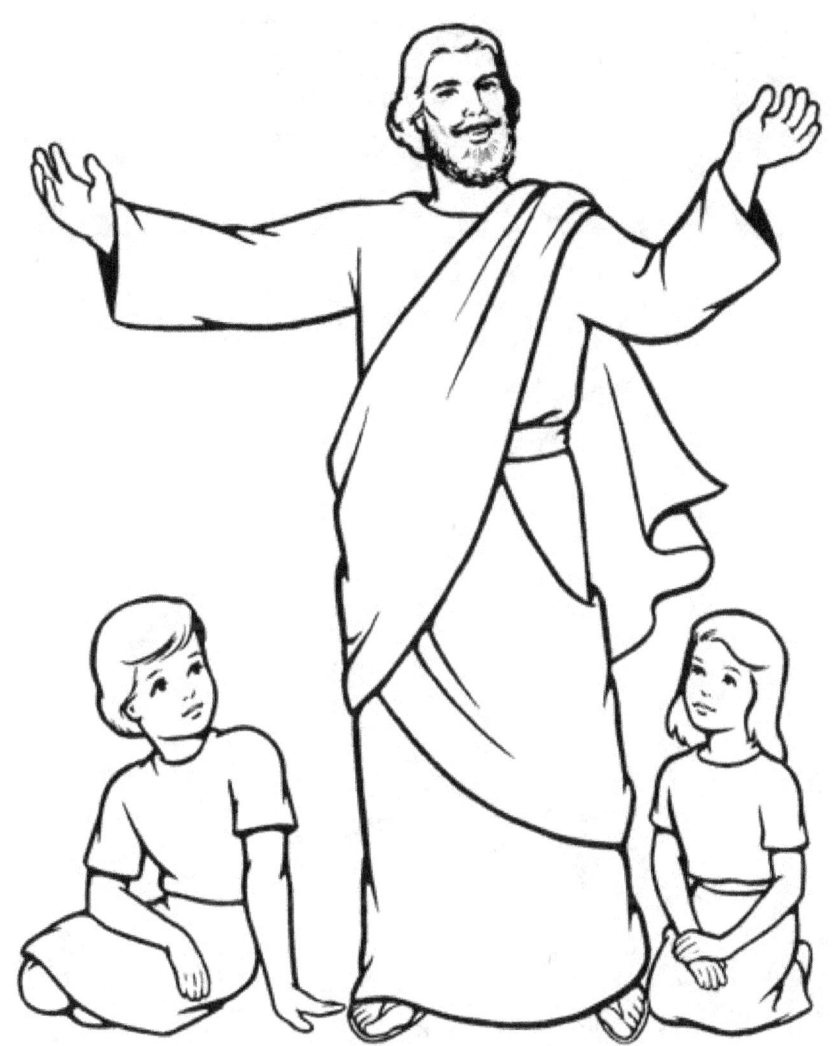

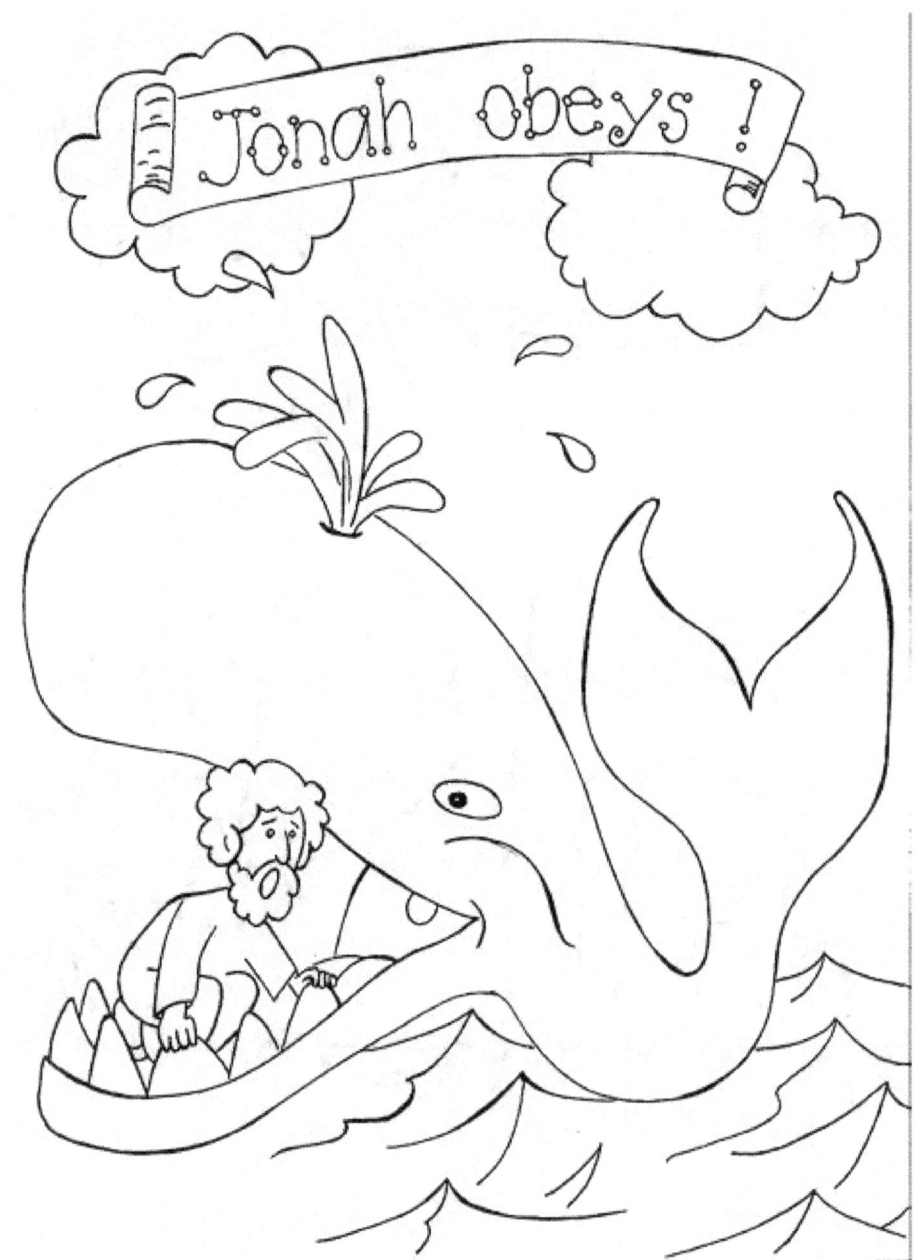

DO NOT BE AFRAID OR DISCOURAGED.

FOR THE LORD YOUR

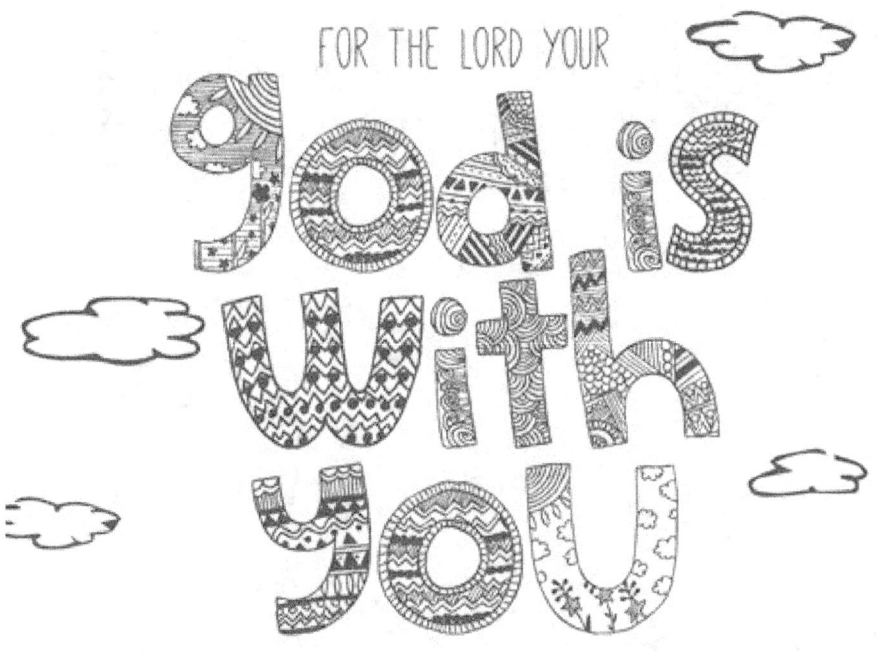

god is
with
you

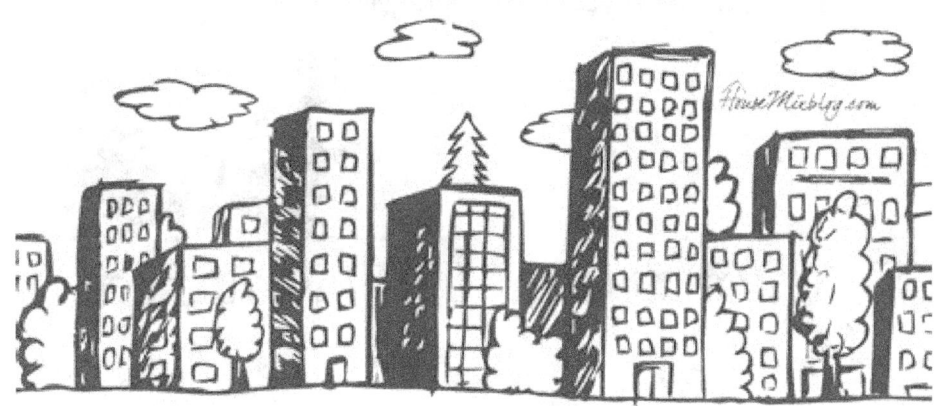

WHEREVER YOU GO. JOSHUA 1:9

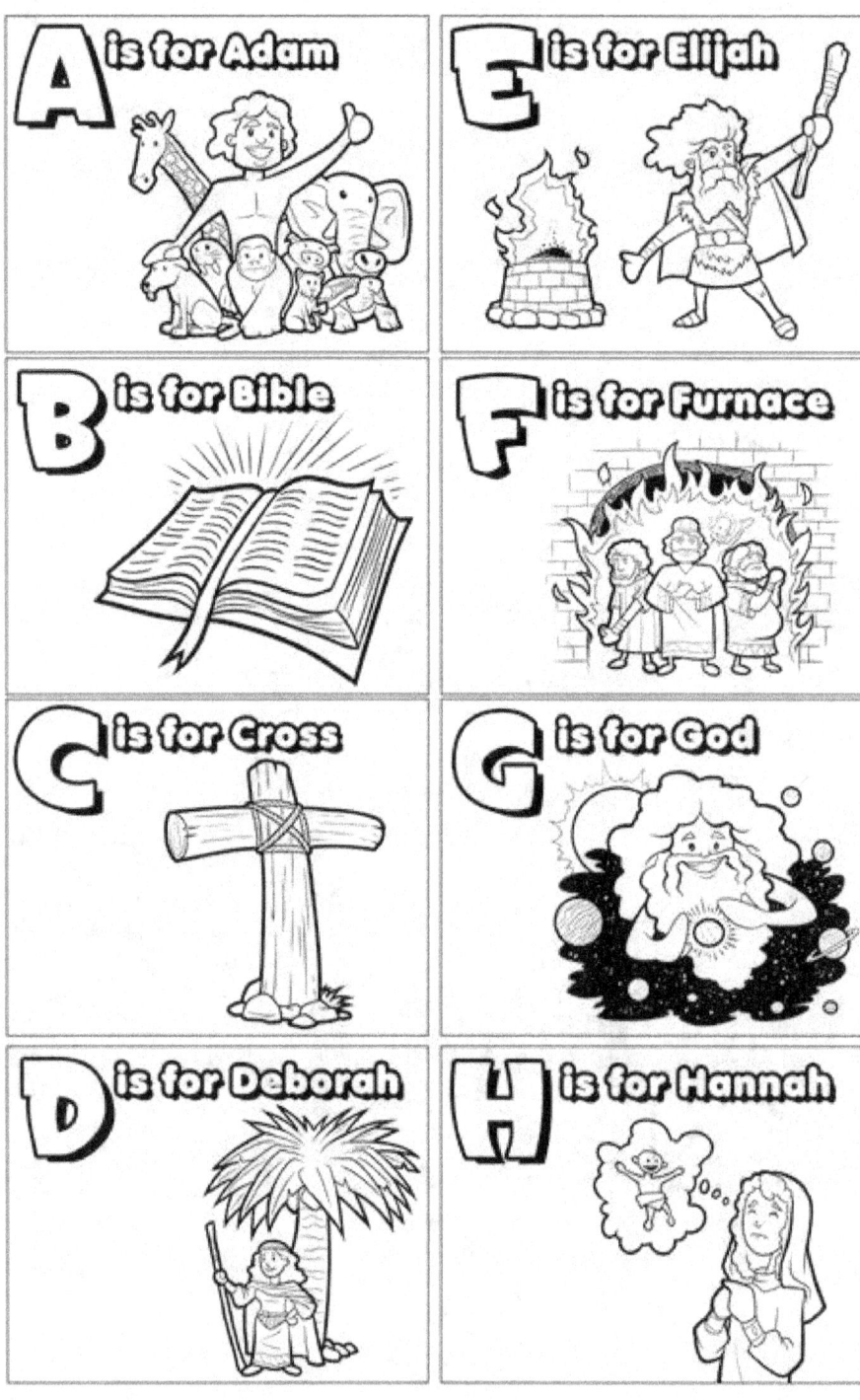

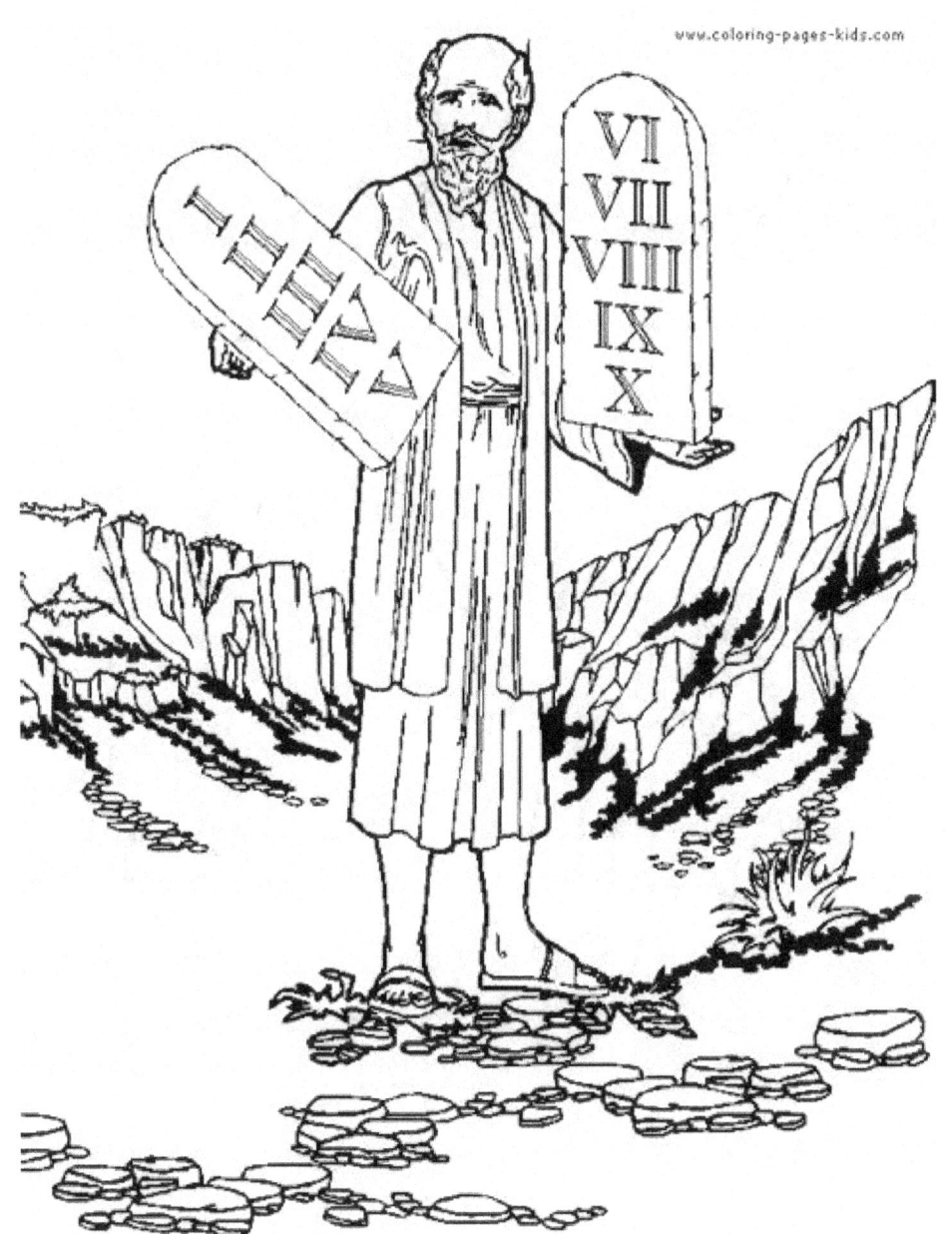

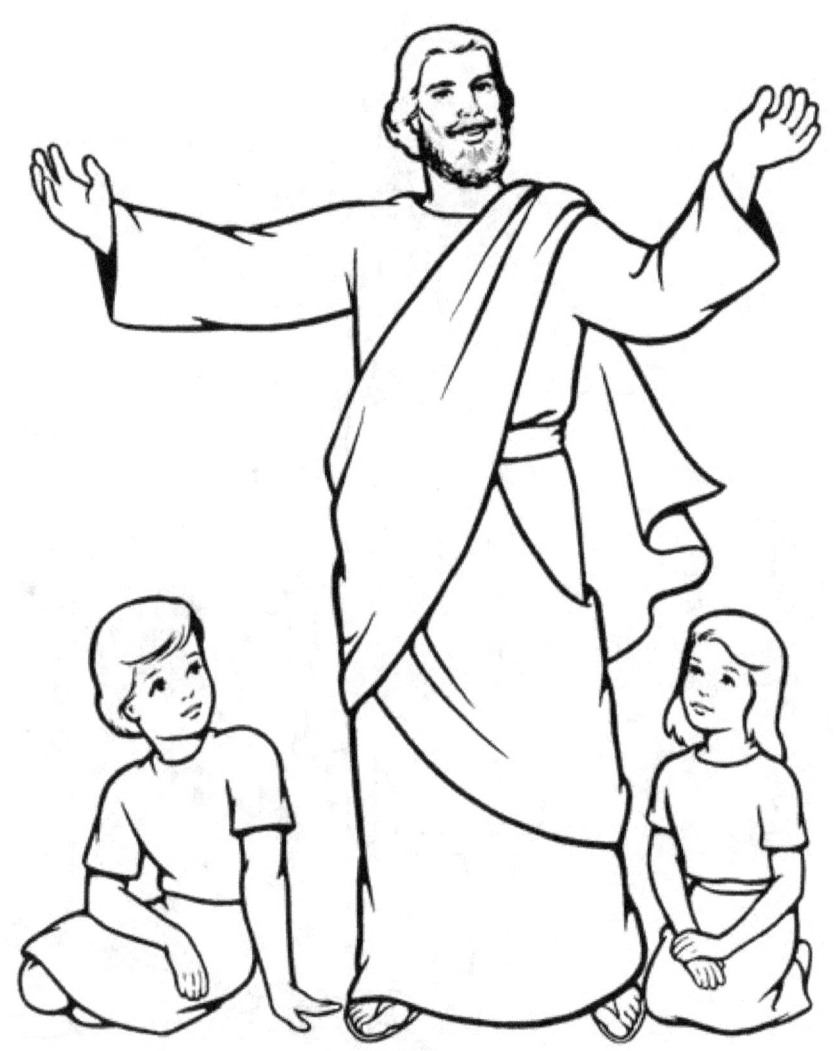

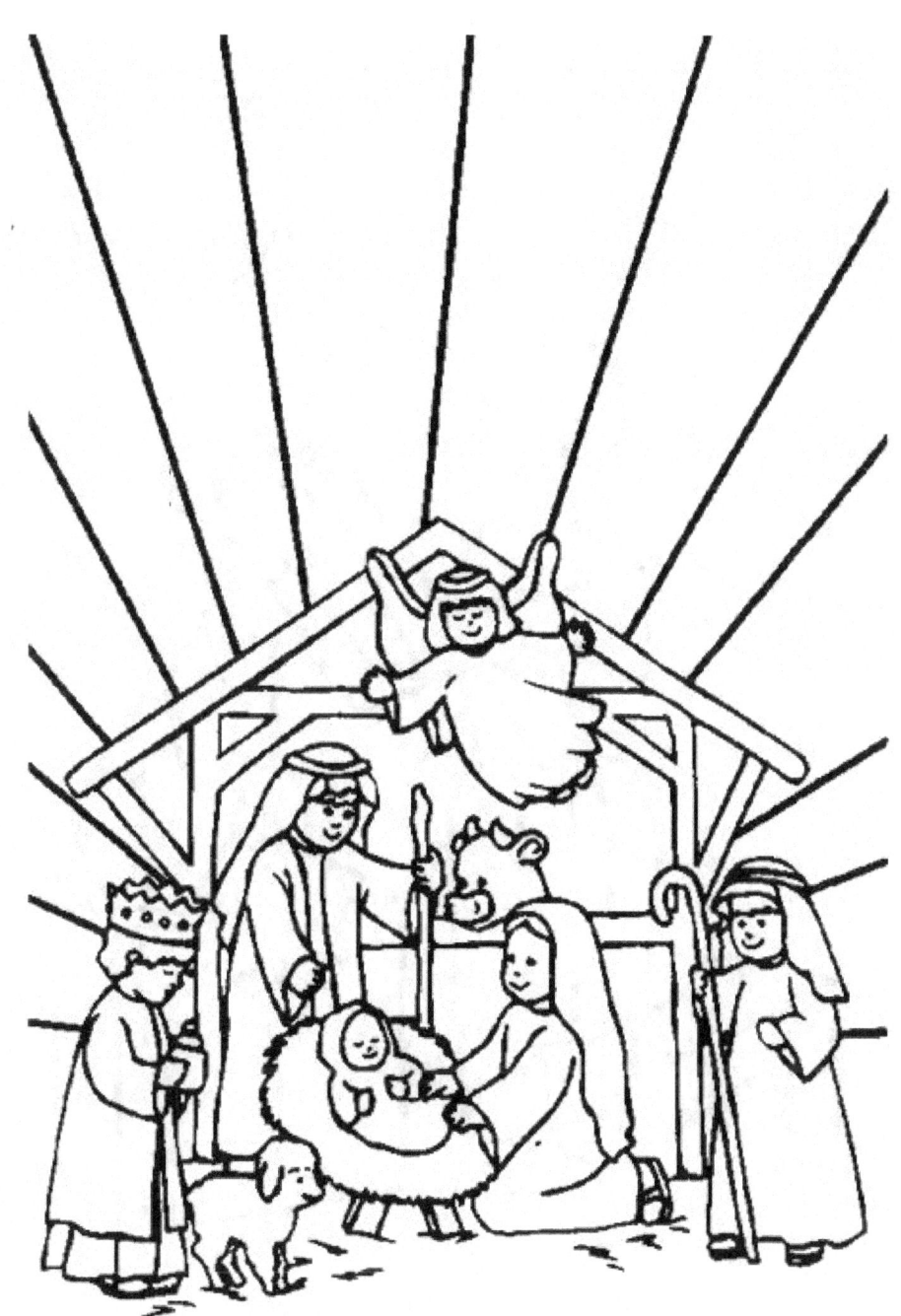

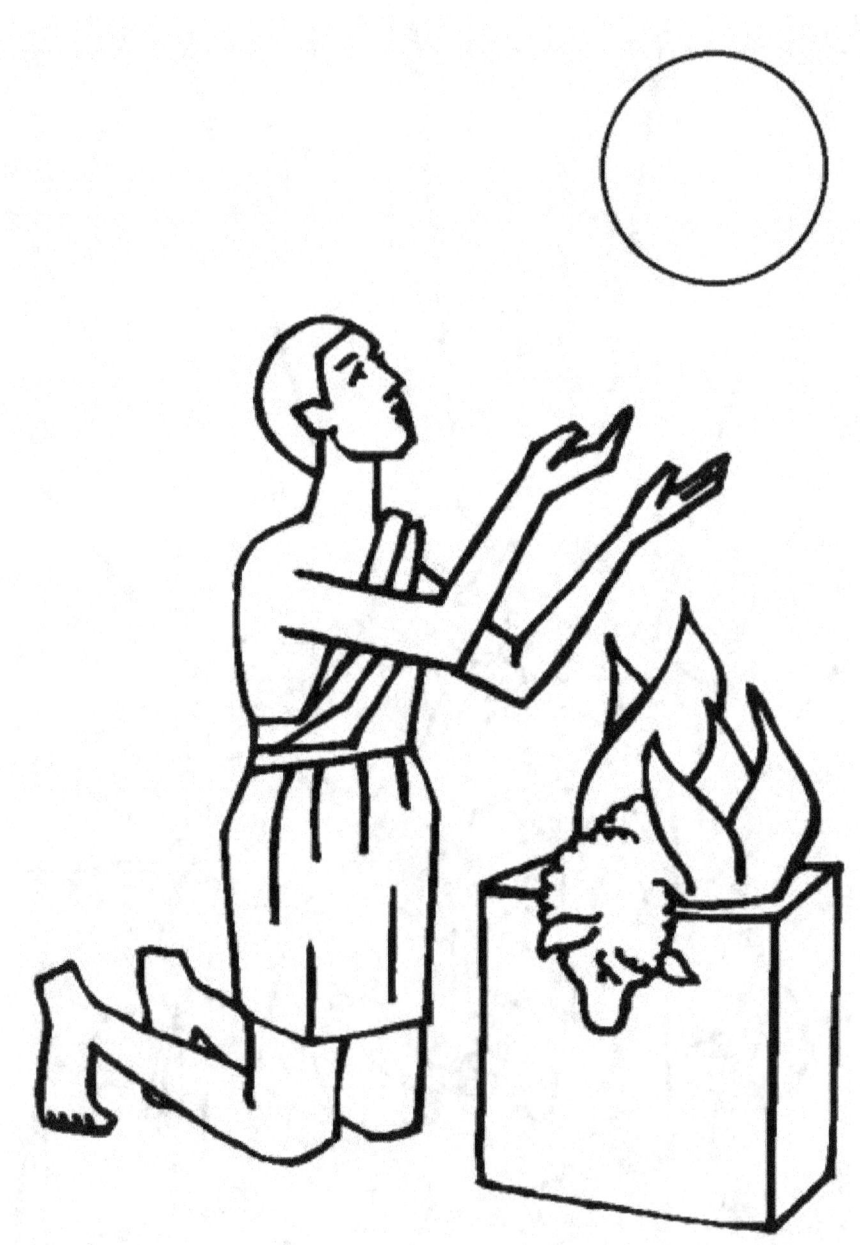

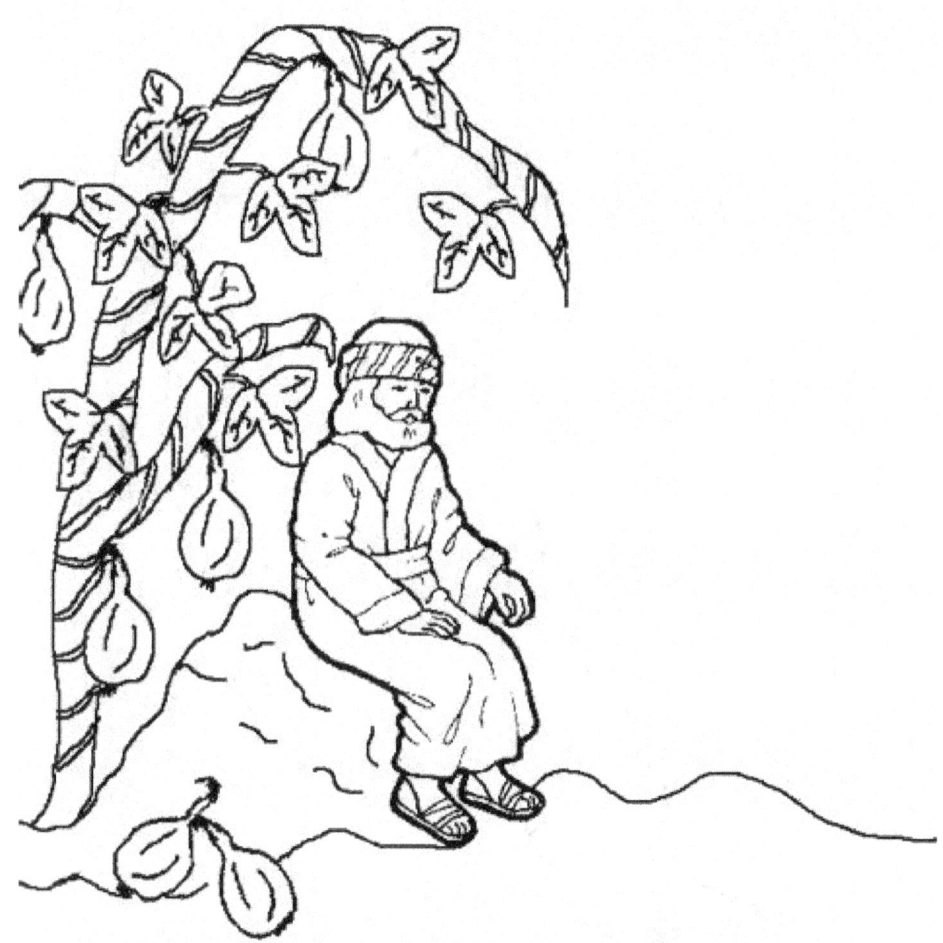

The Lord is not willing that any
should perish, but that all should come
to repentance. 2 Peter 3:9b

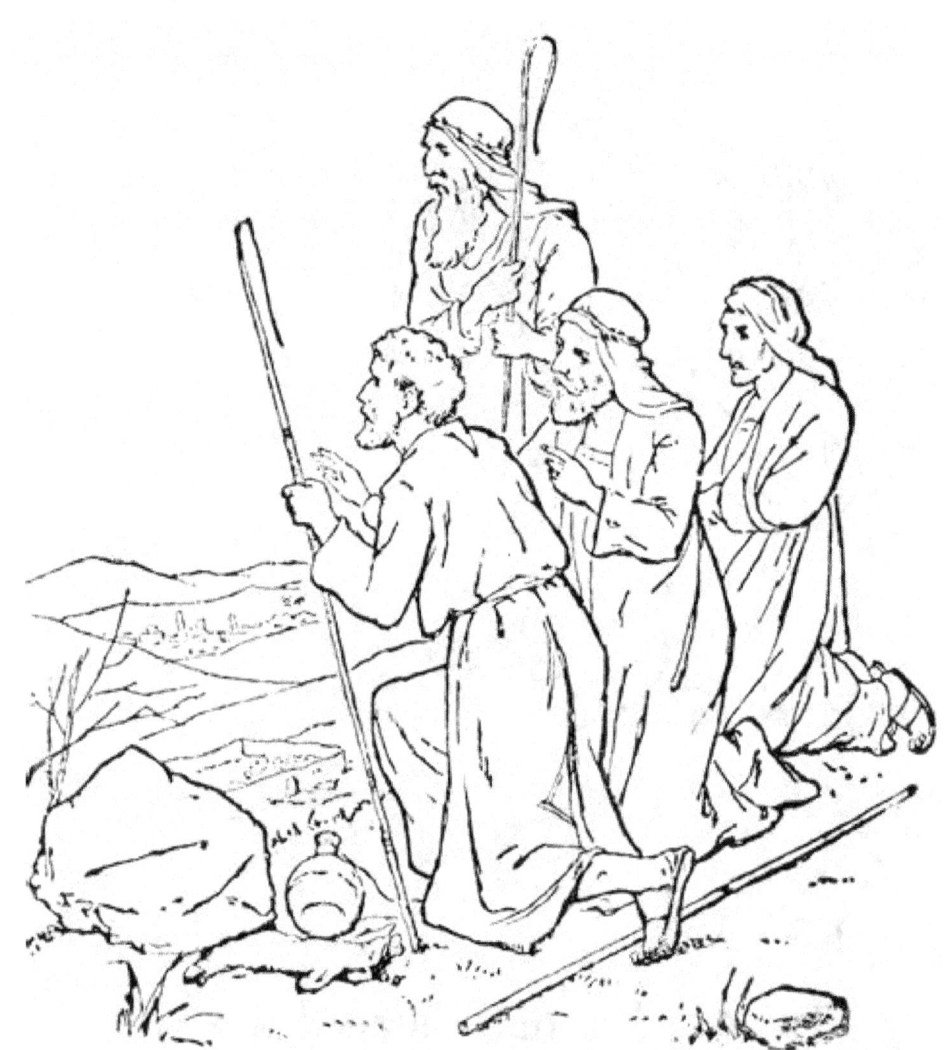

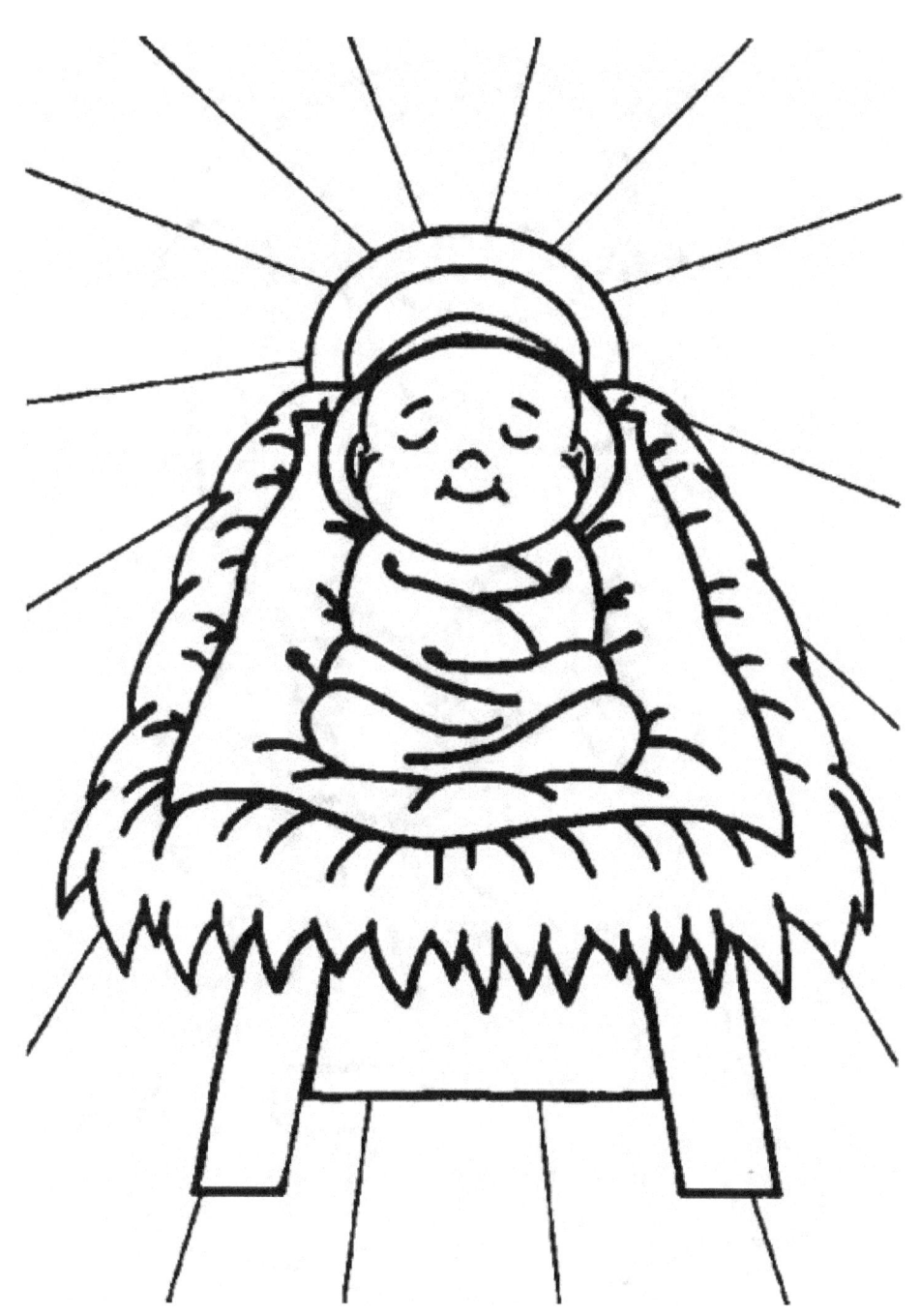

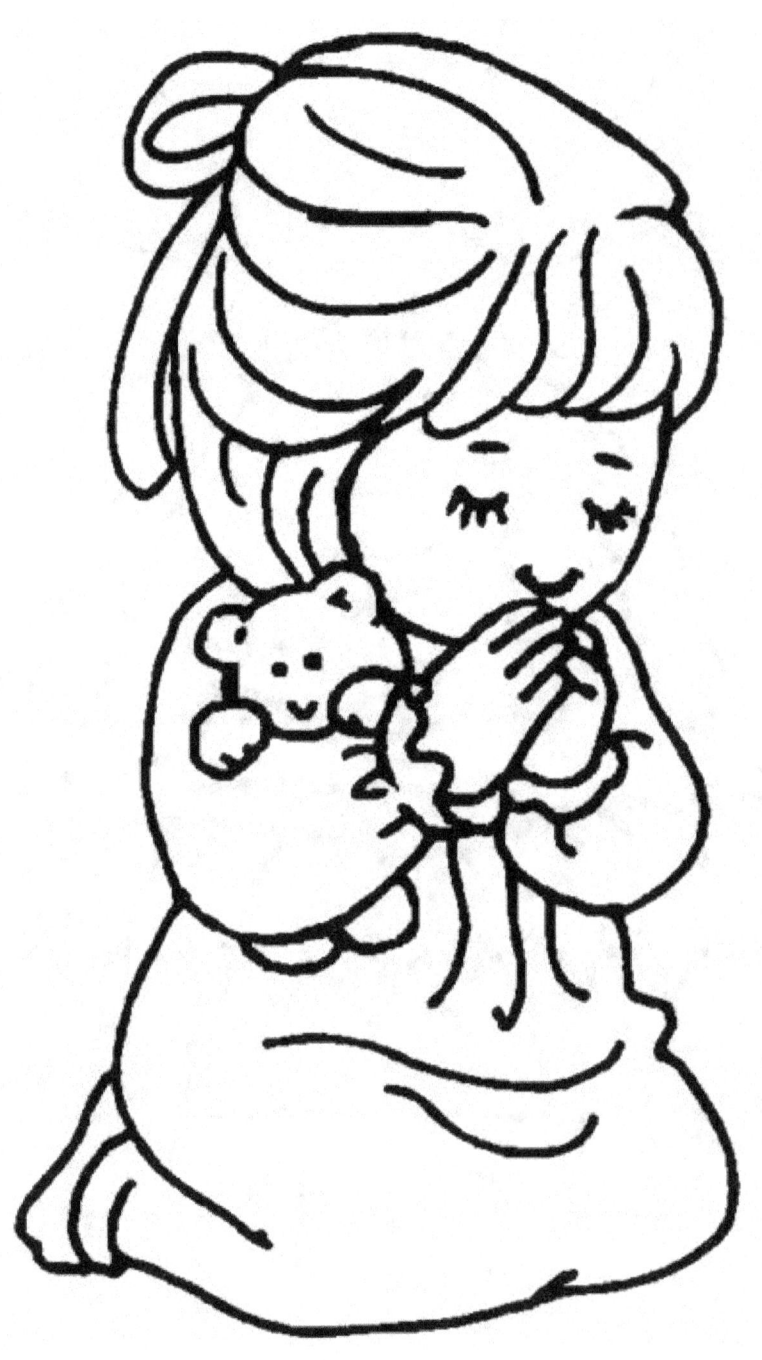

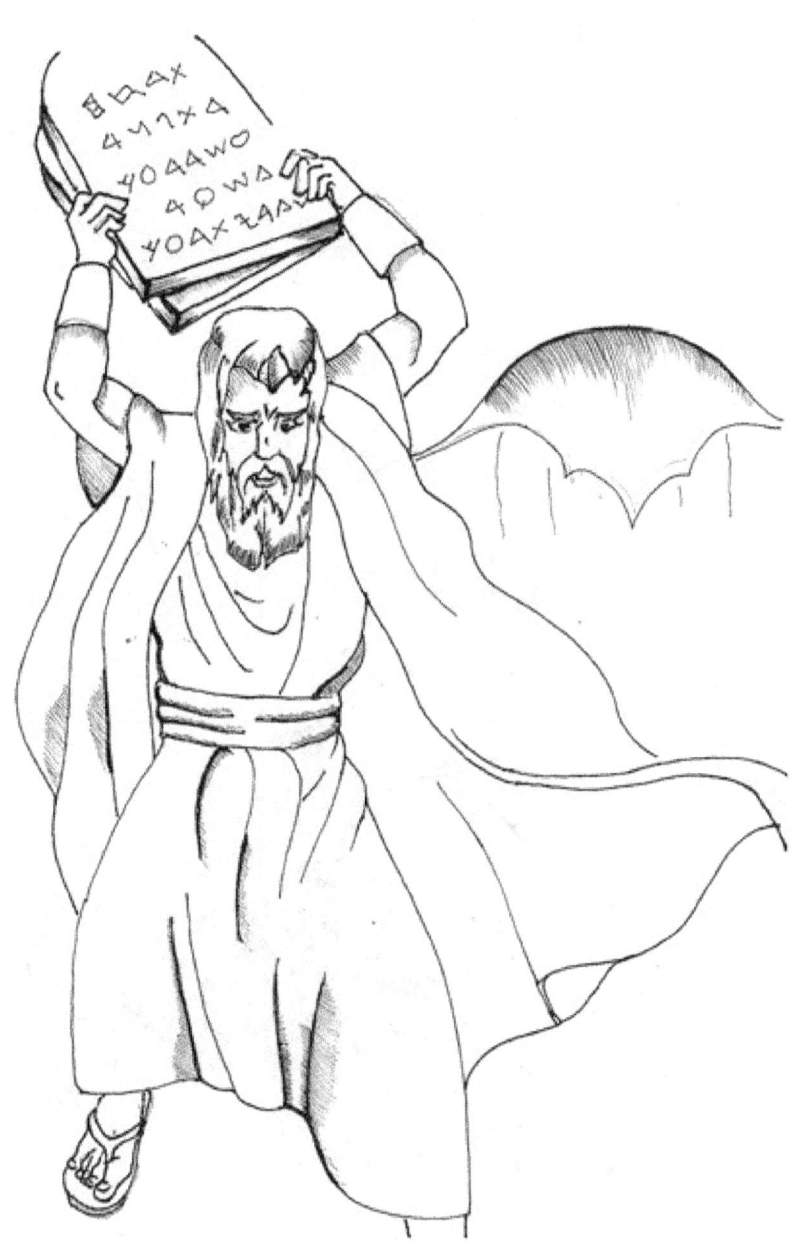

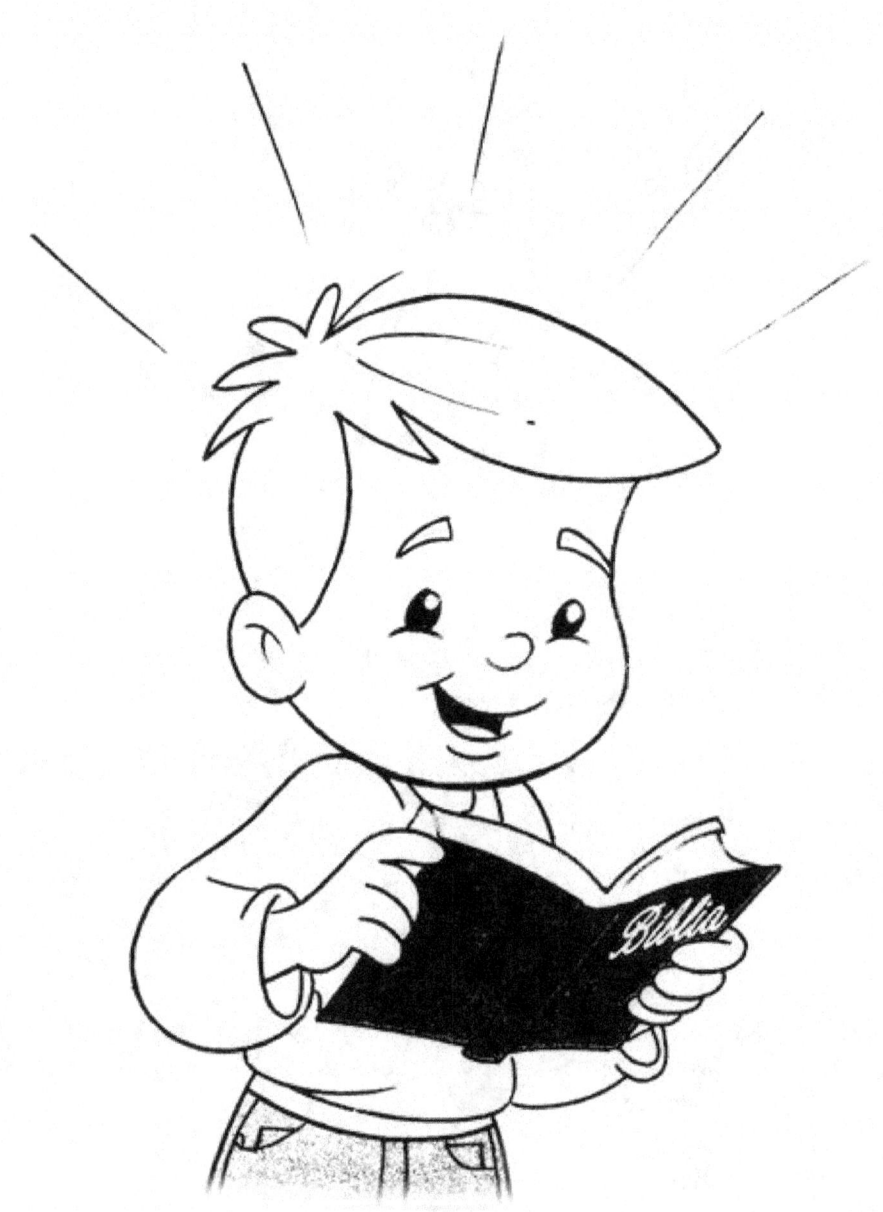

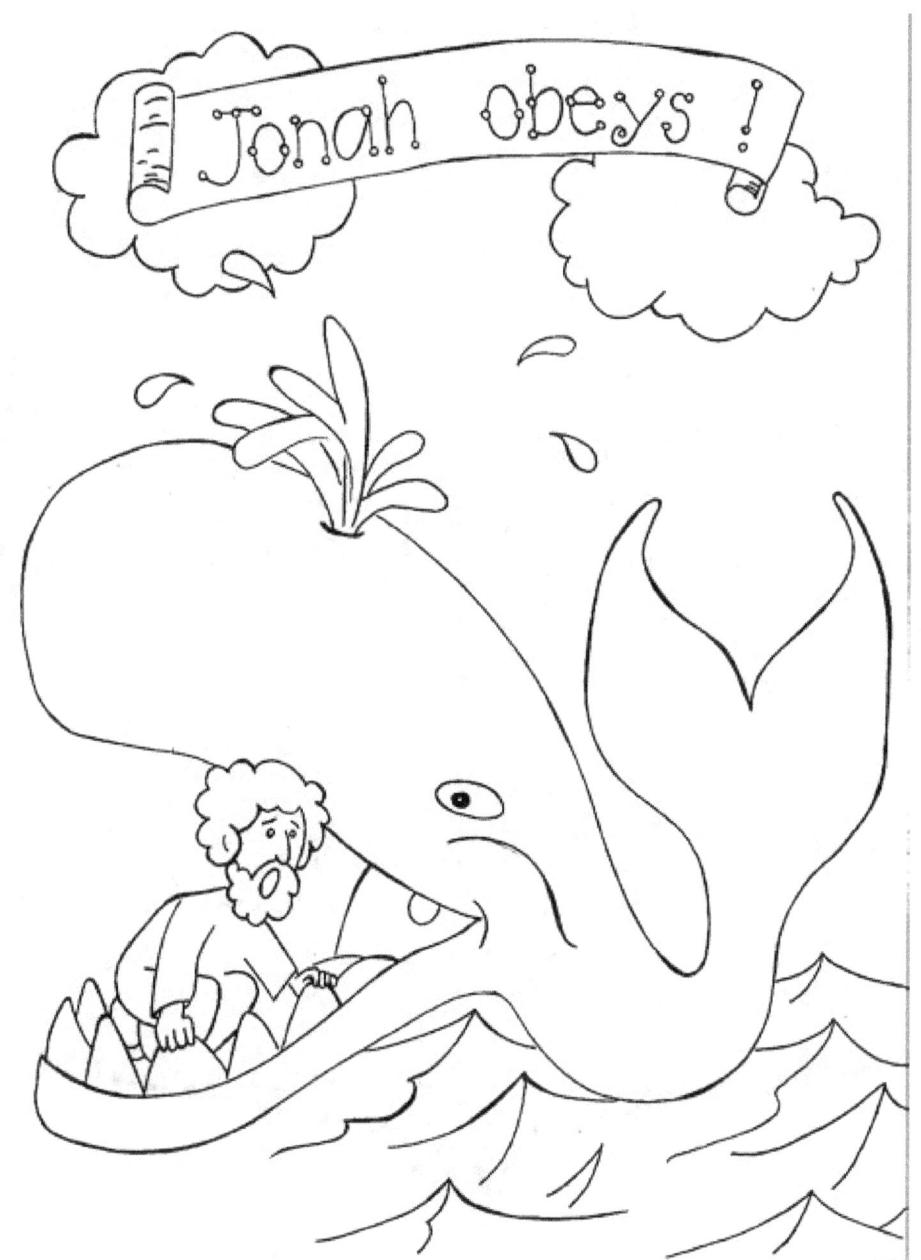

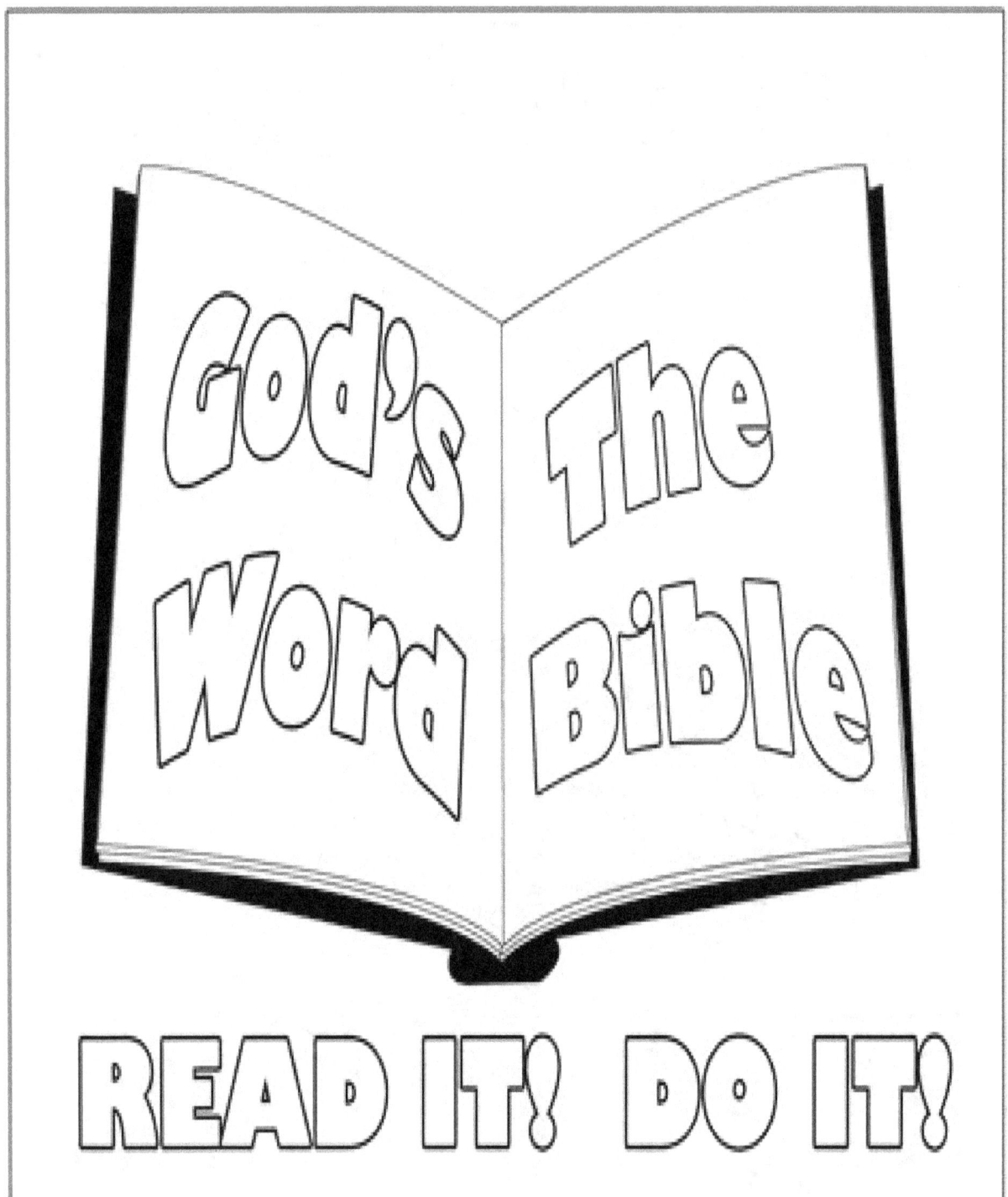

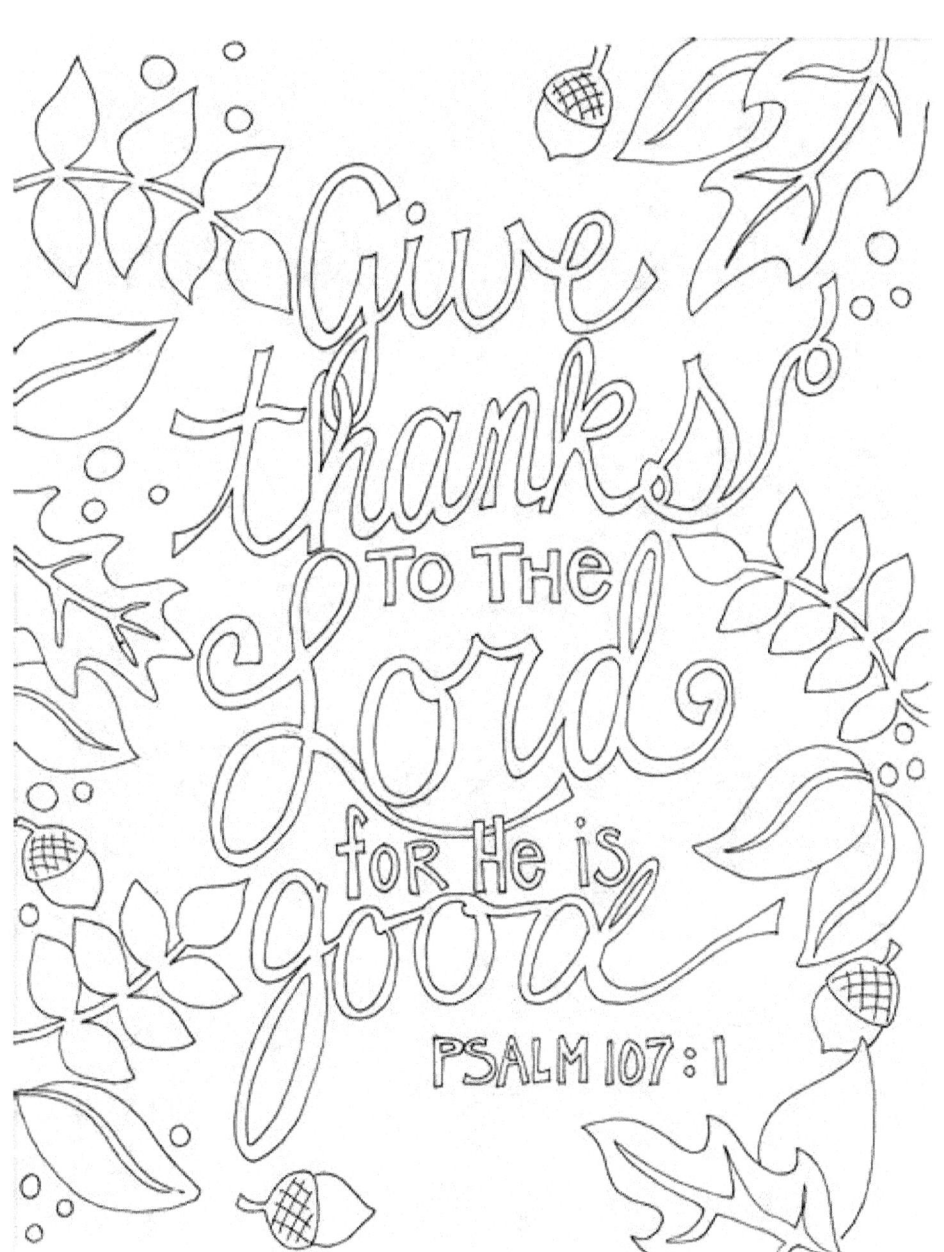

Give thanks TO THE Lord for He is good

PSALM 107:1

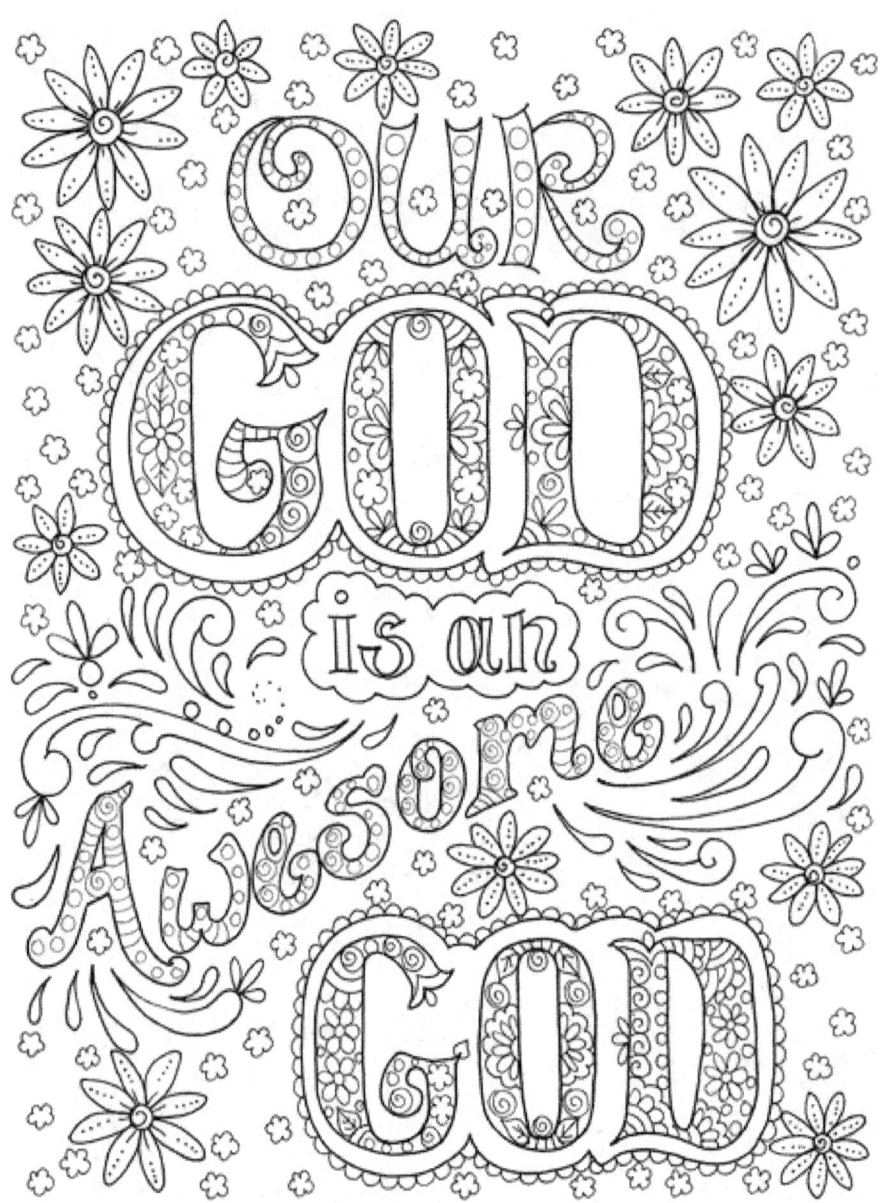

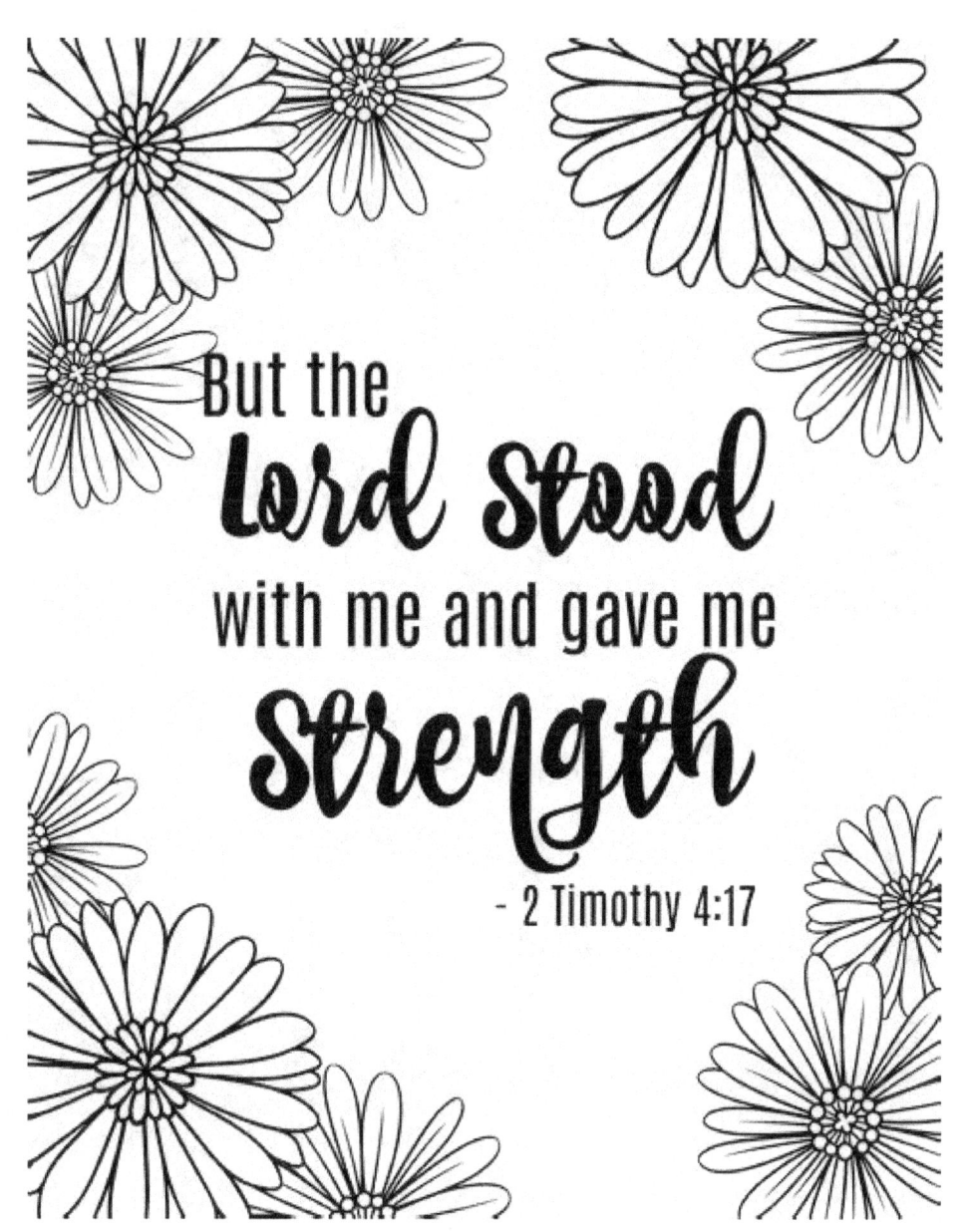

But the
Lord stood
with me and gave me
strength

- 2 Timothy 4:17

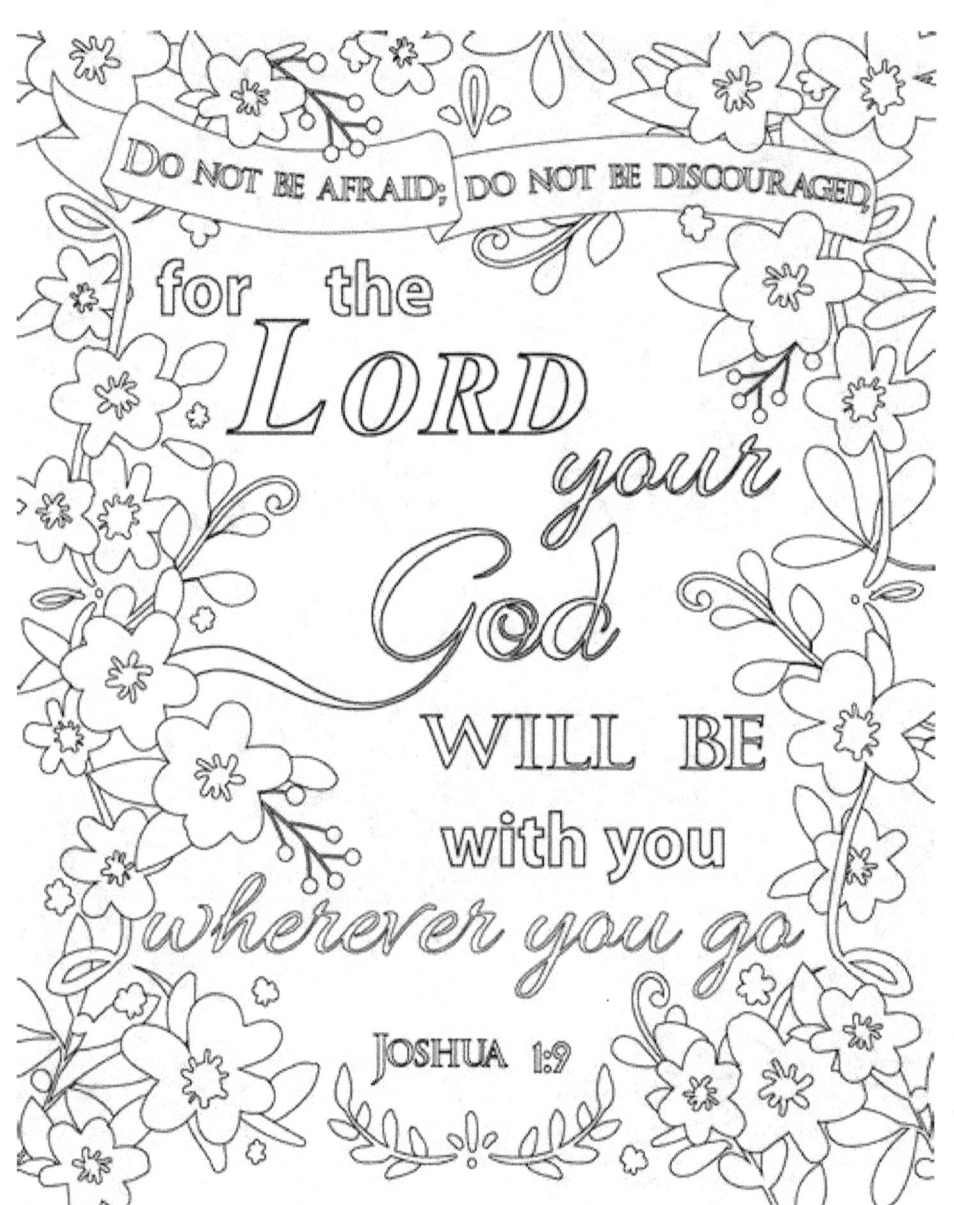

Do not be afraid; do not be discouraged, for the Lord your God will be with you wherever you go

Joshua 1:9

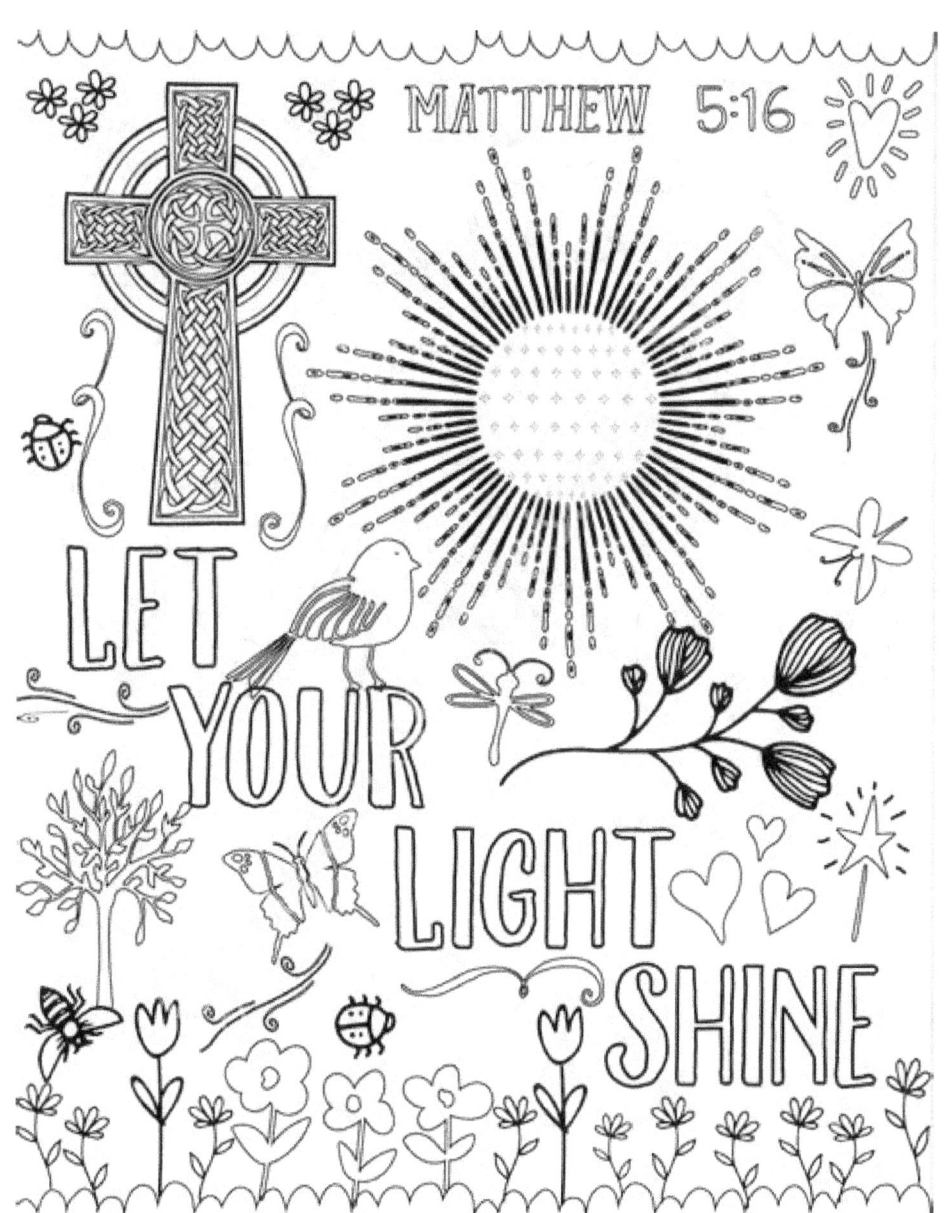

MATTHEW 5:16

LET YOUR LIGHT SHINE

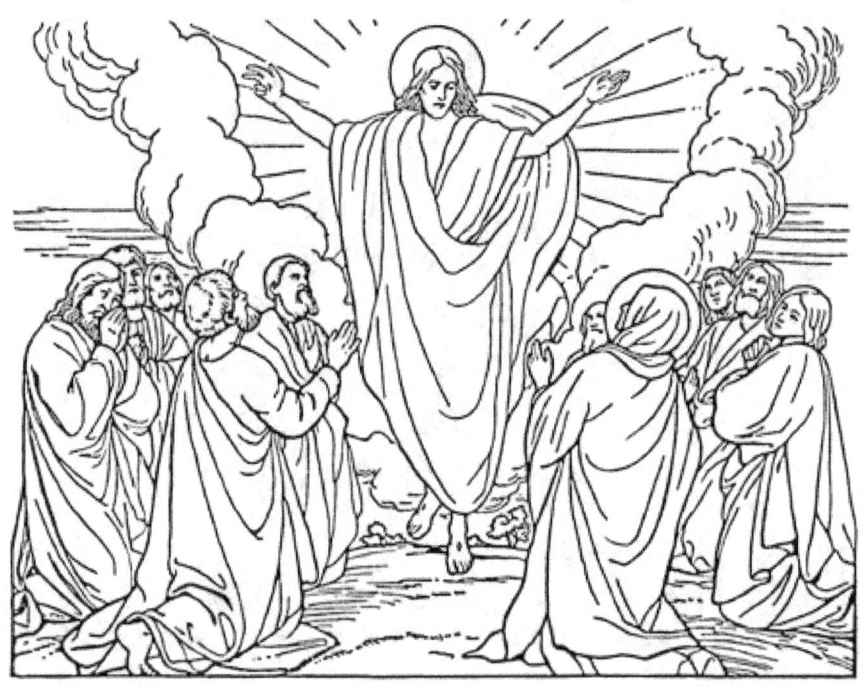

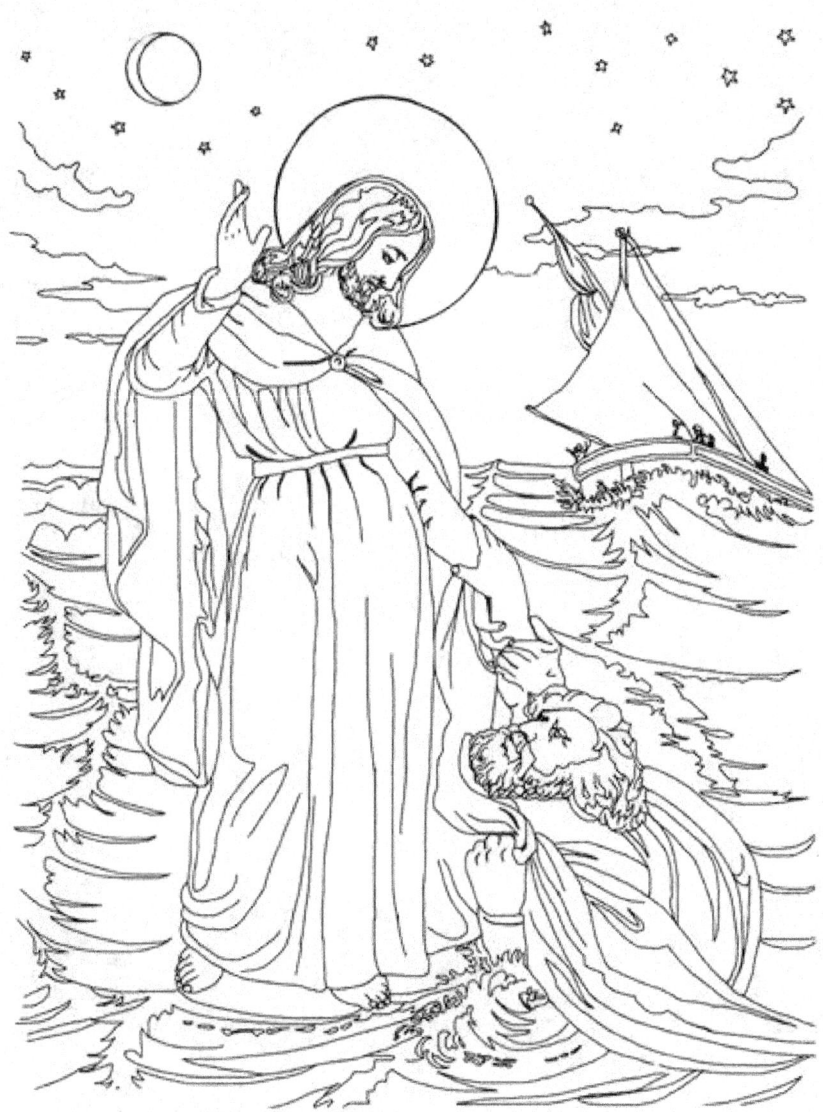

Christ Walking on the Sea

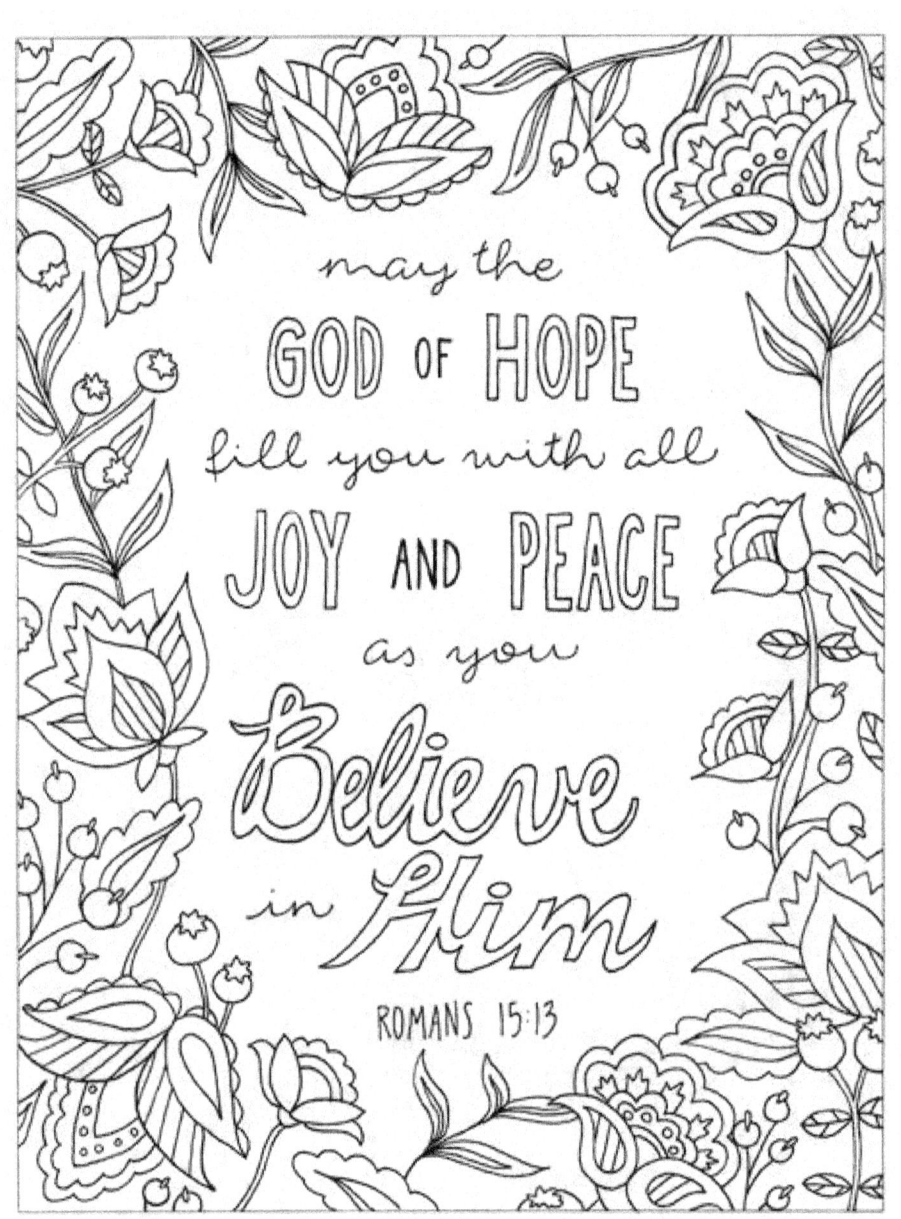

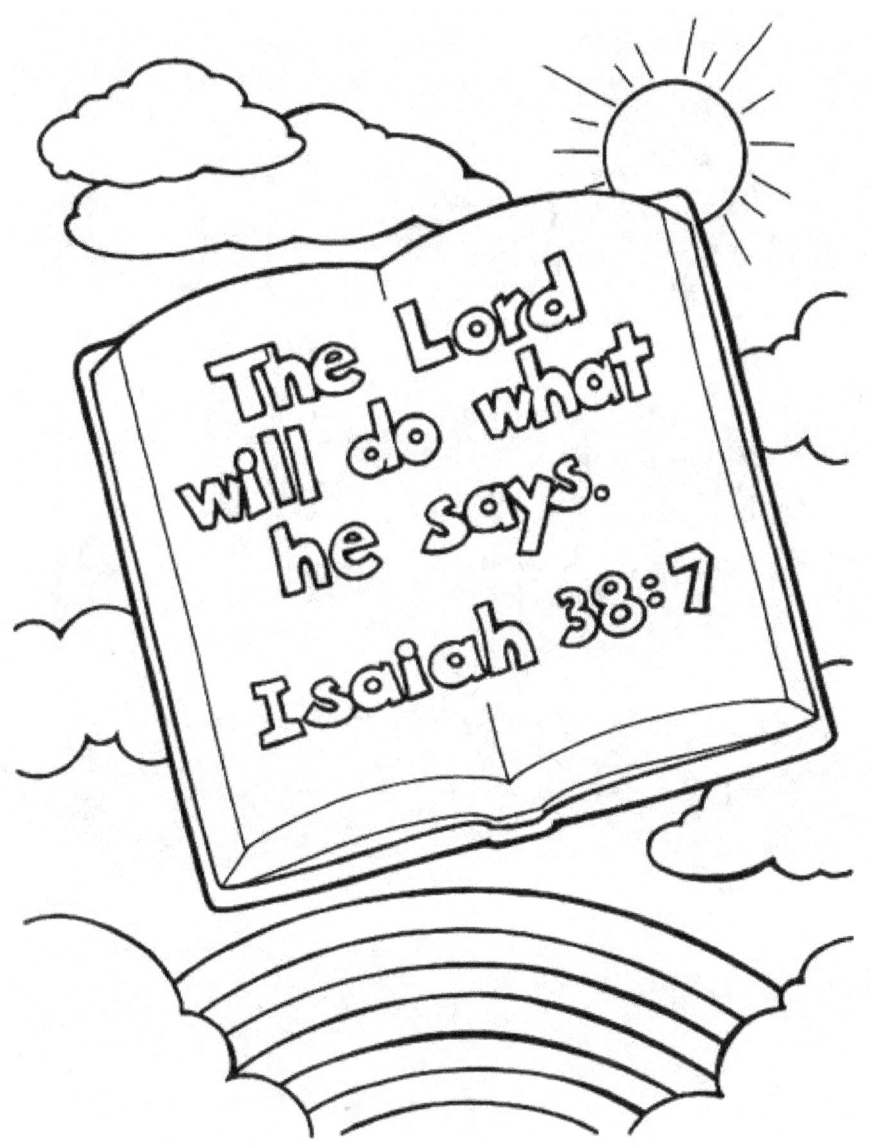

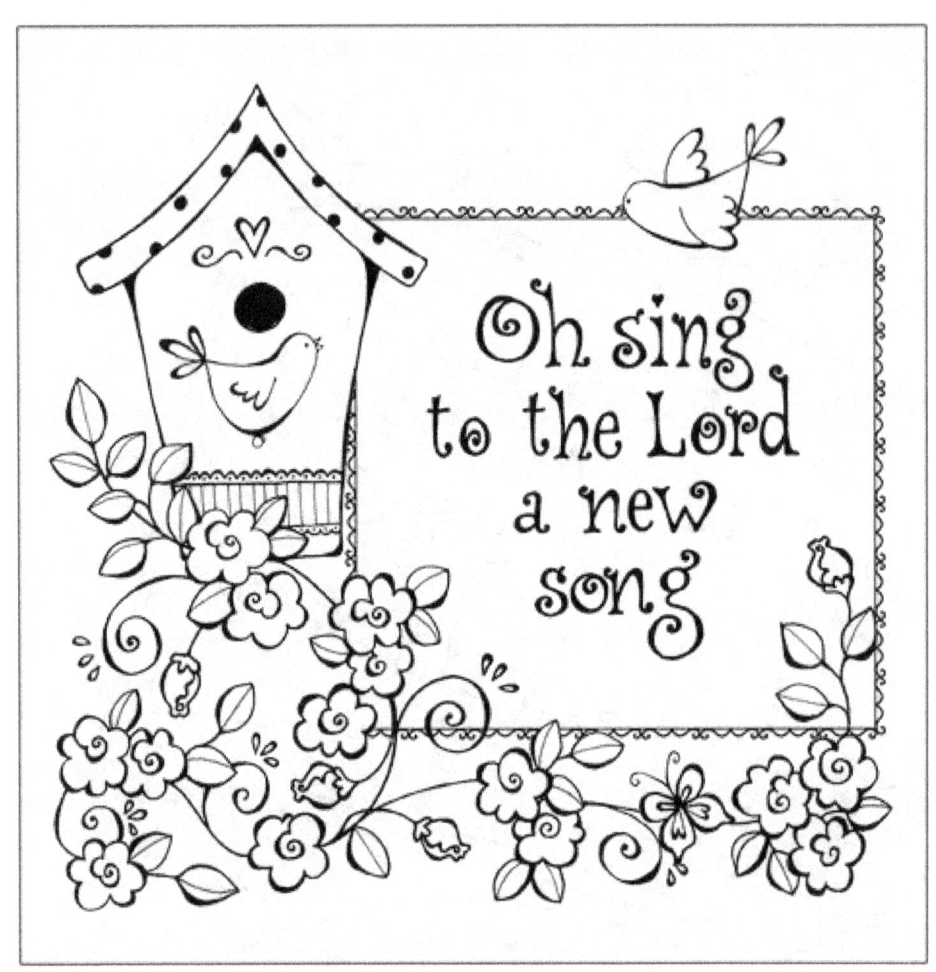

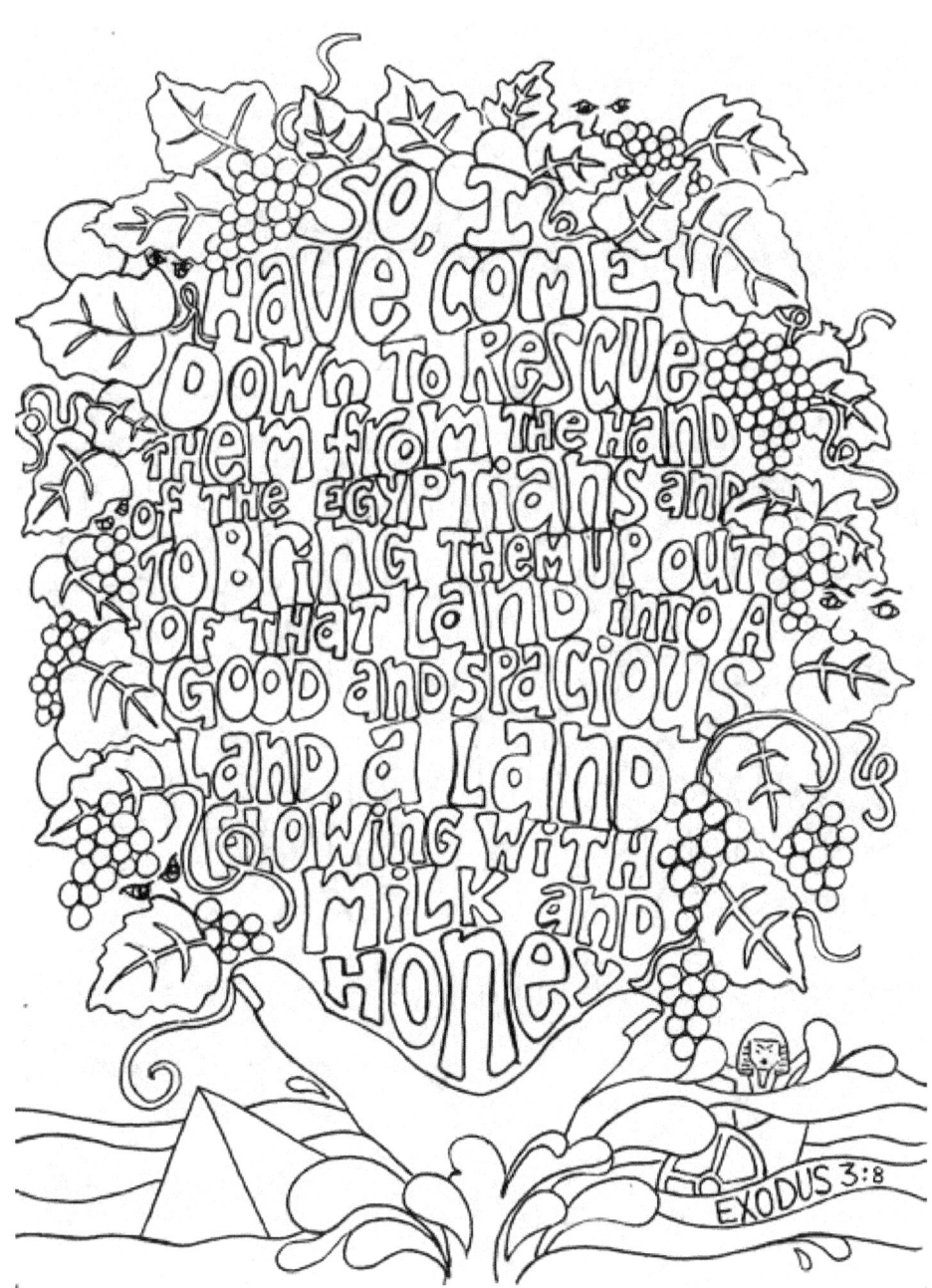

SO, I HAVE COME DOWN TO RESCUE THEM FROM THE HAND OF THE EGYPTIANS AND TO BRING THEM UP OUT OF THAT LAND INTO A GOOD AND SPACIOUS LAND A LAND FLOWING WITH MILK AND HONEY

EXODUS 3:8

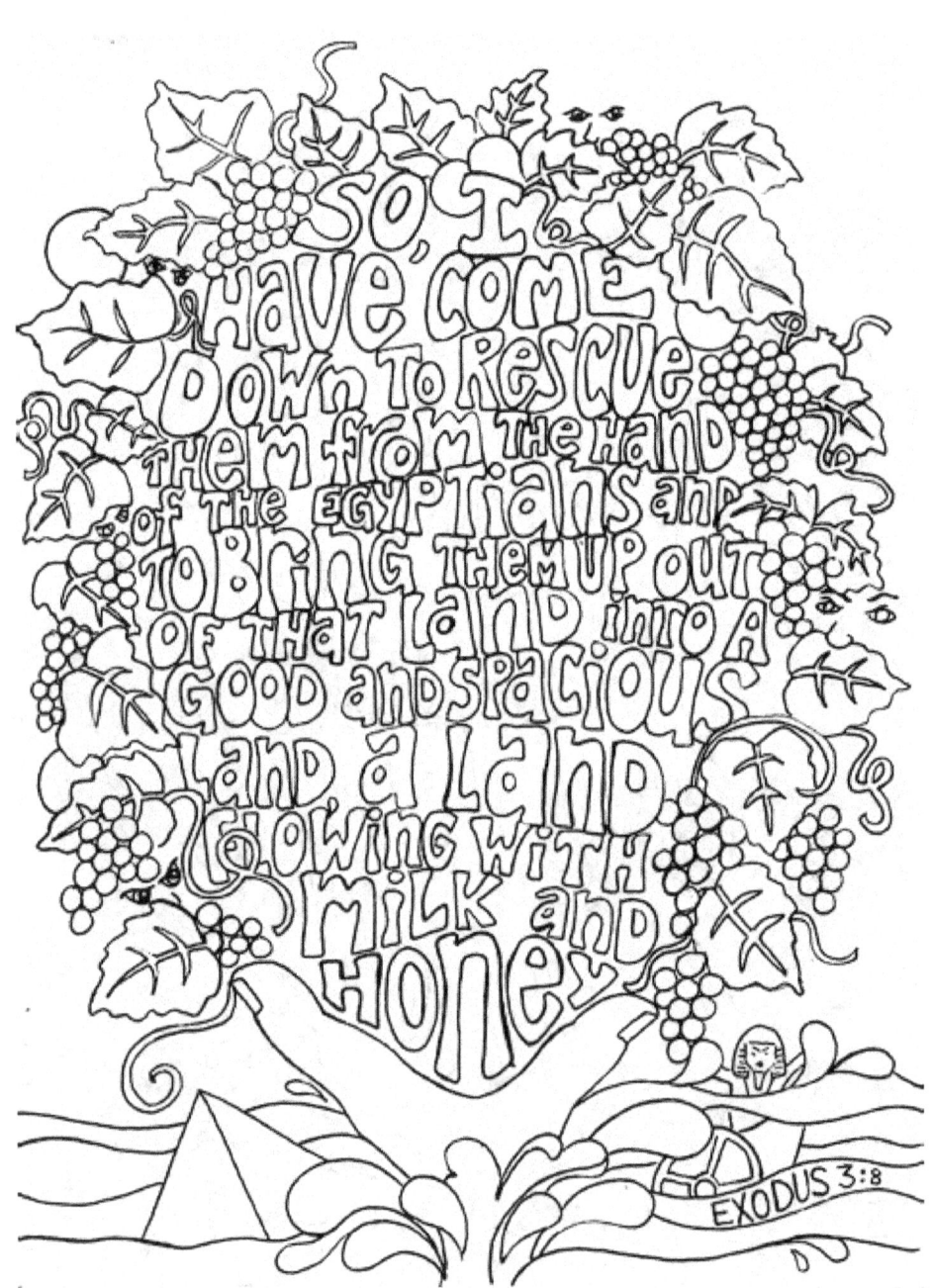

SO, I HAVE COME DOWN TO RESCUE THEM FROM THE HAND OF THE EGYPTIANS AND TO BRING THEM UP OUT OF THAT LAND INTO A GOOD AND SPACIOUS LAND, A LAND FLOWING WITH MILK AND HONEY

EXODUS 3:8

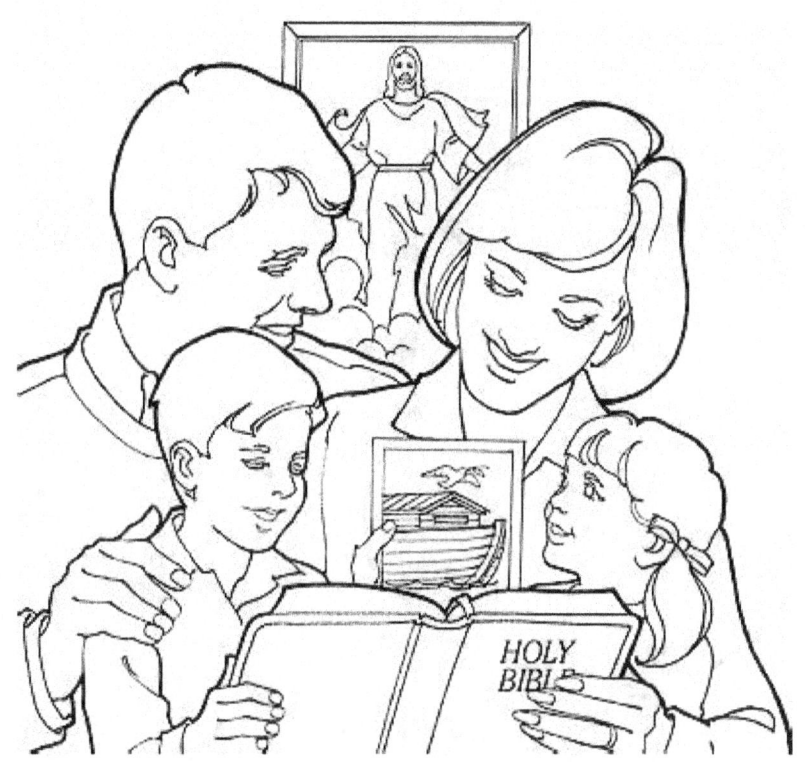

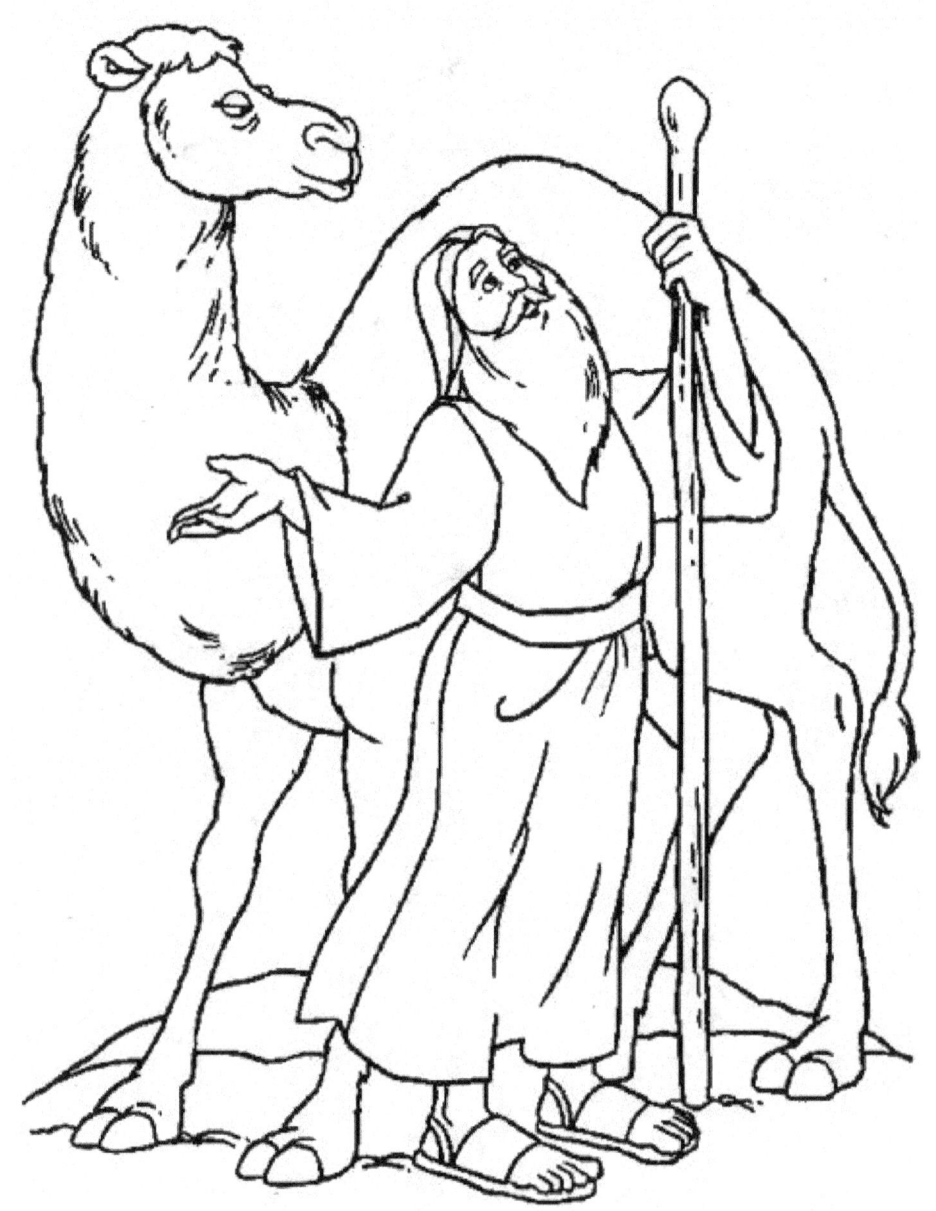

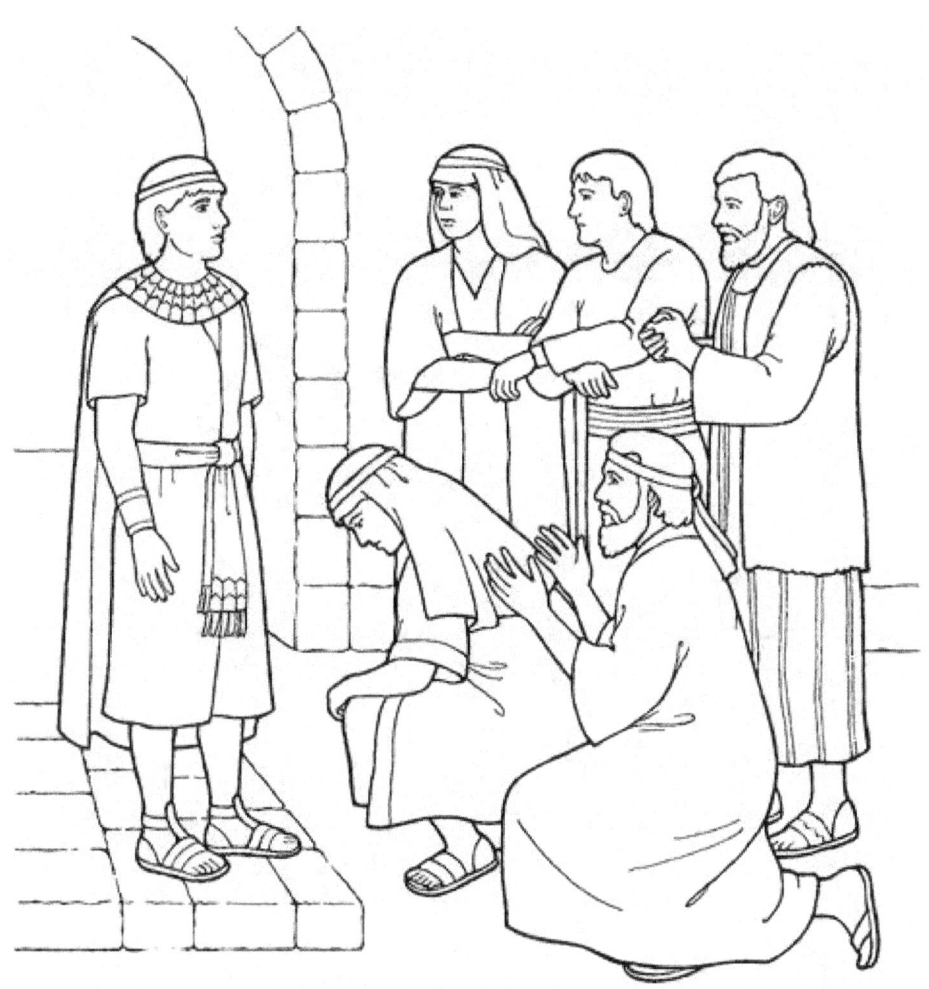

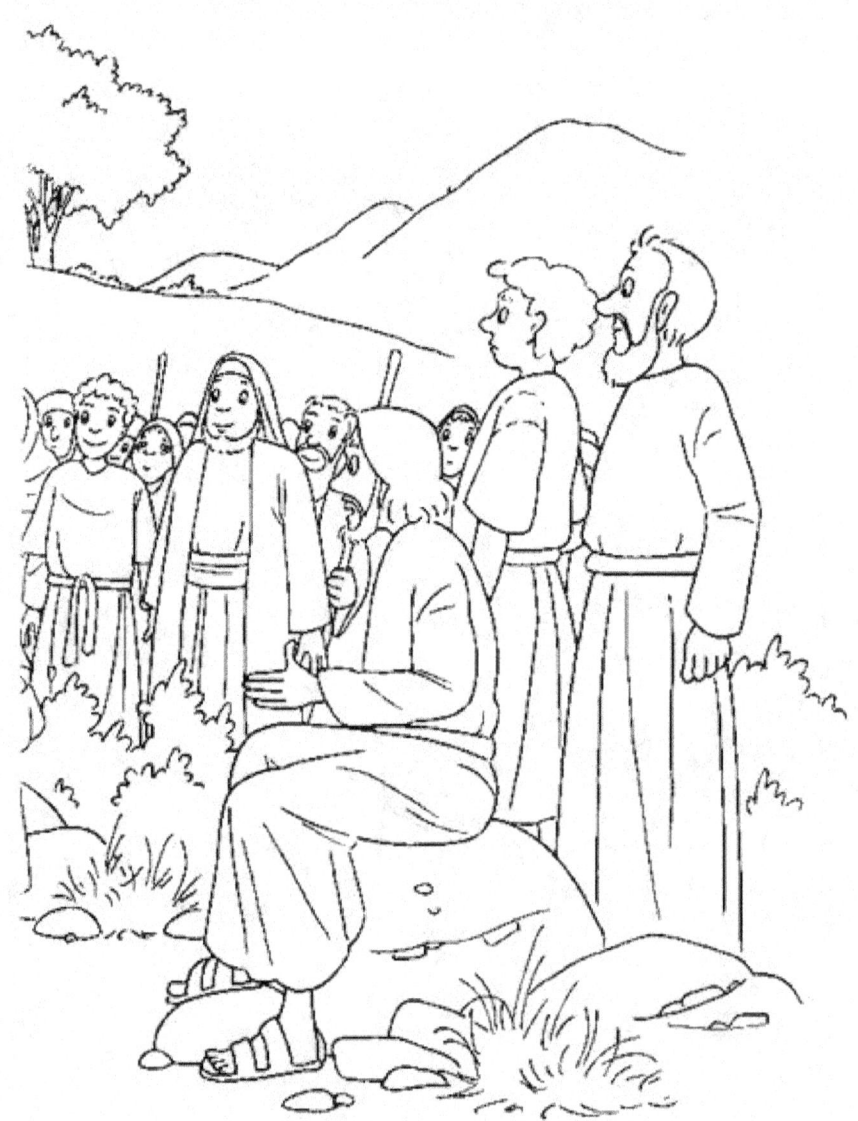

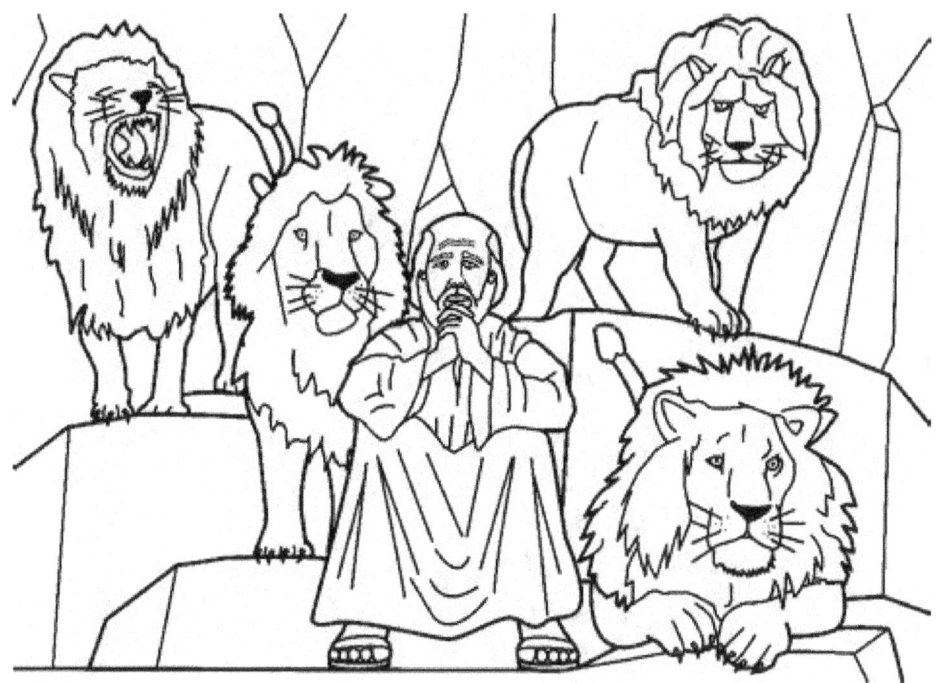

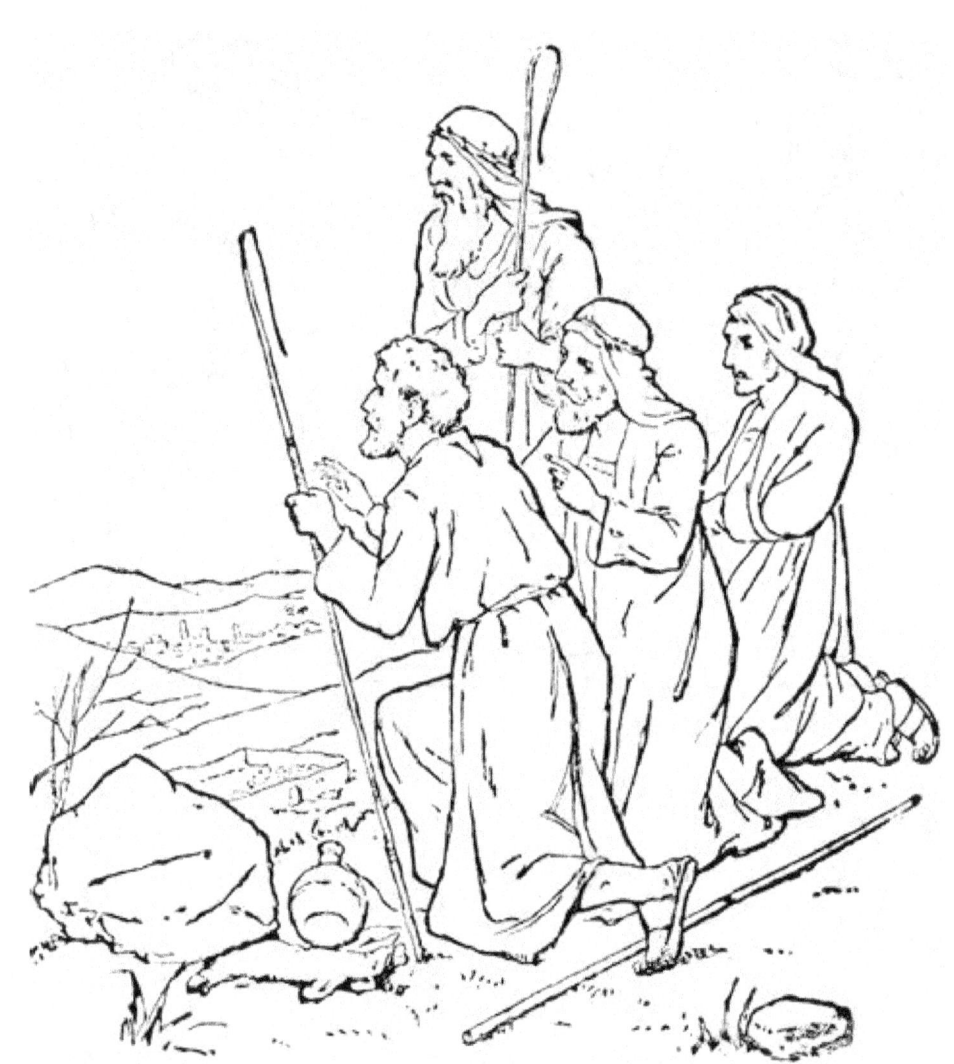

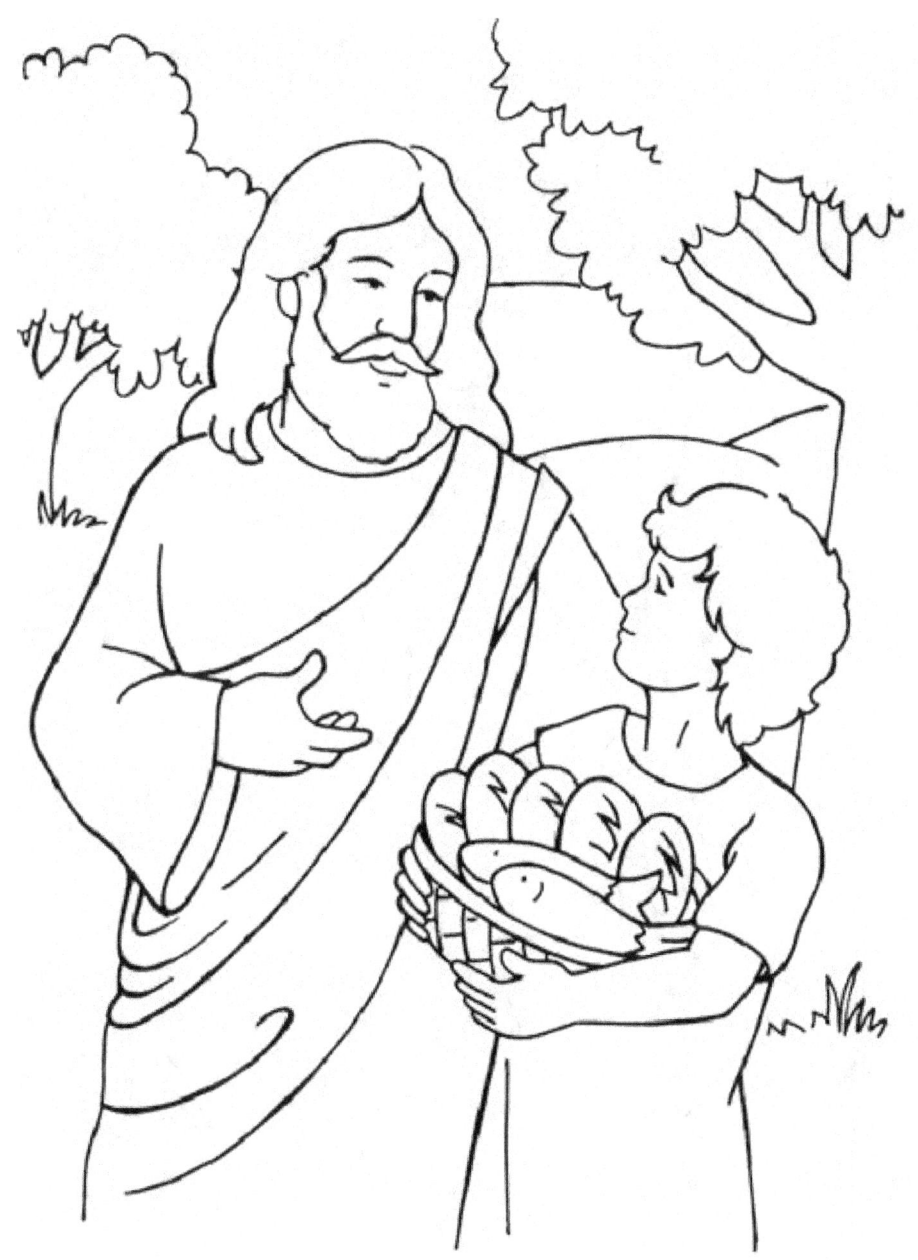

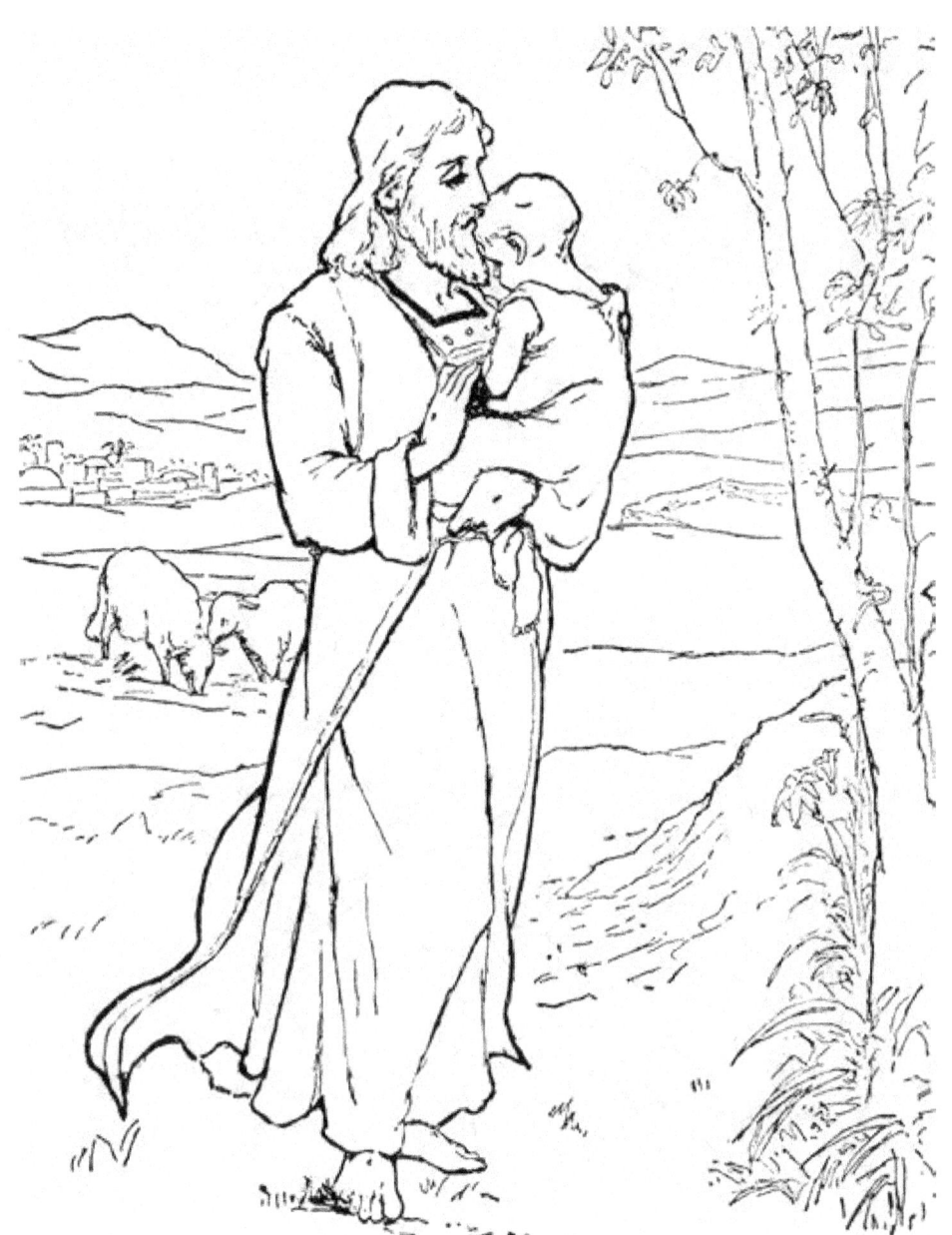

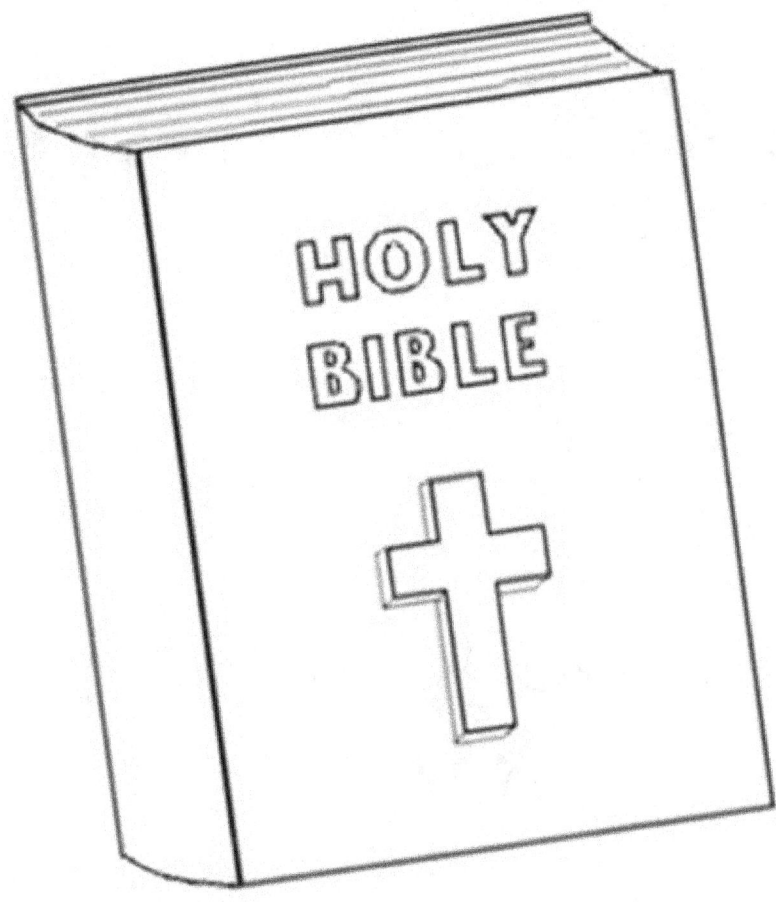

I Love God's Word

This is
the day
that the
Lord has
made.

-Psalm 118:24

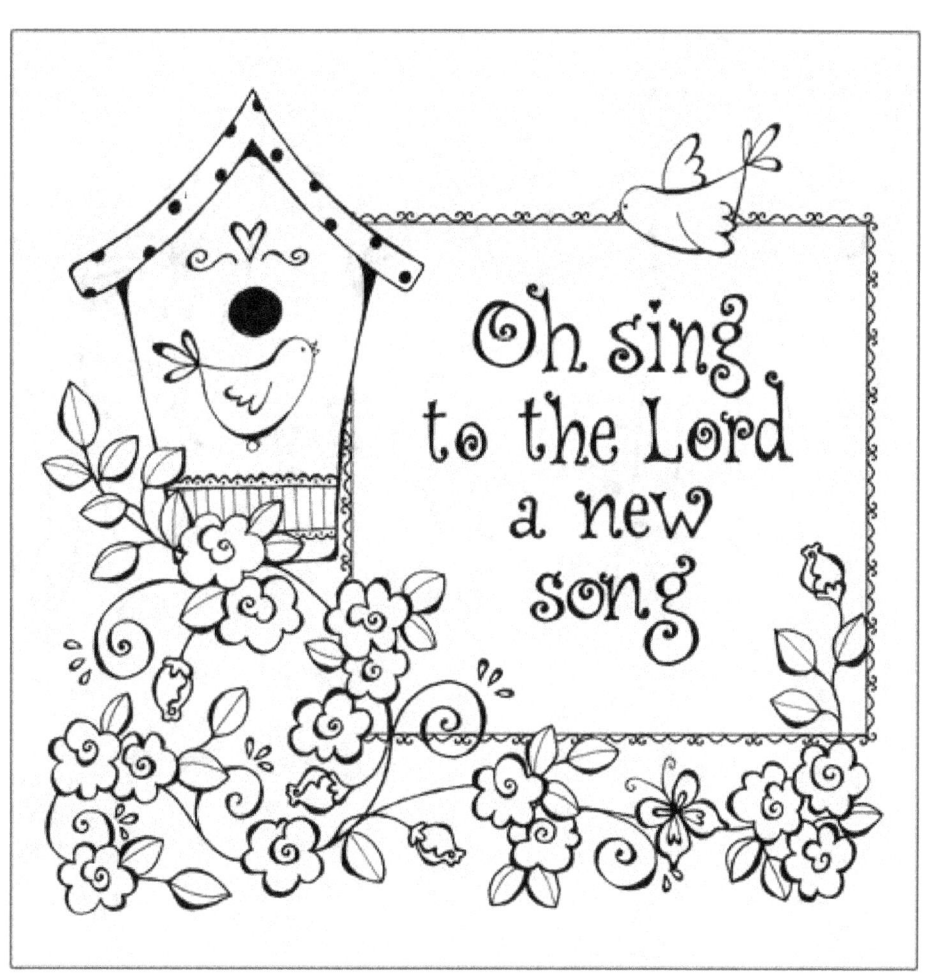

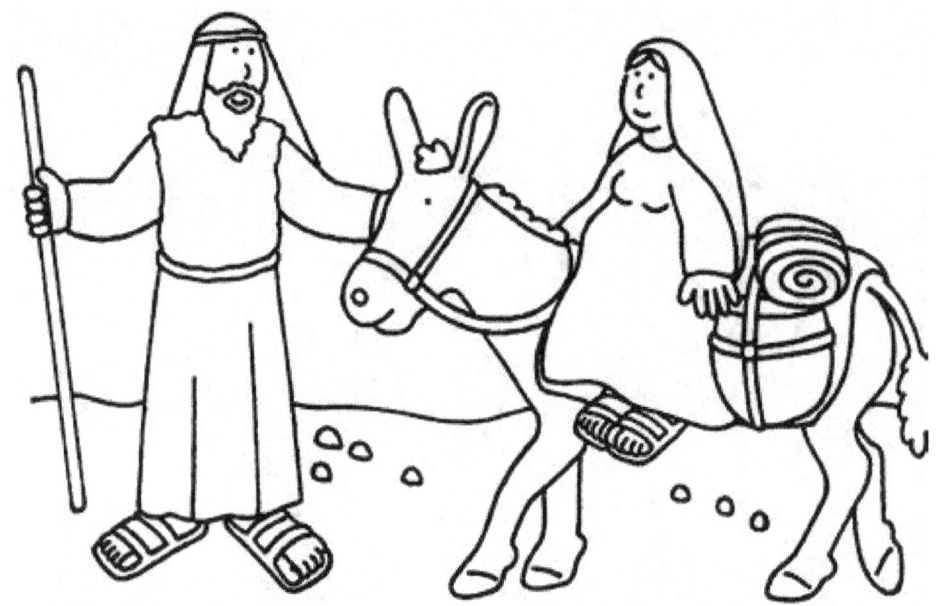

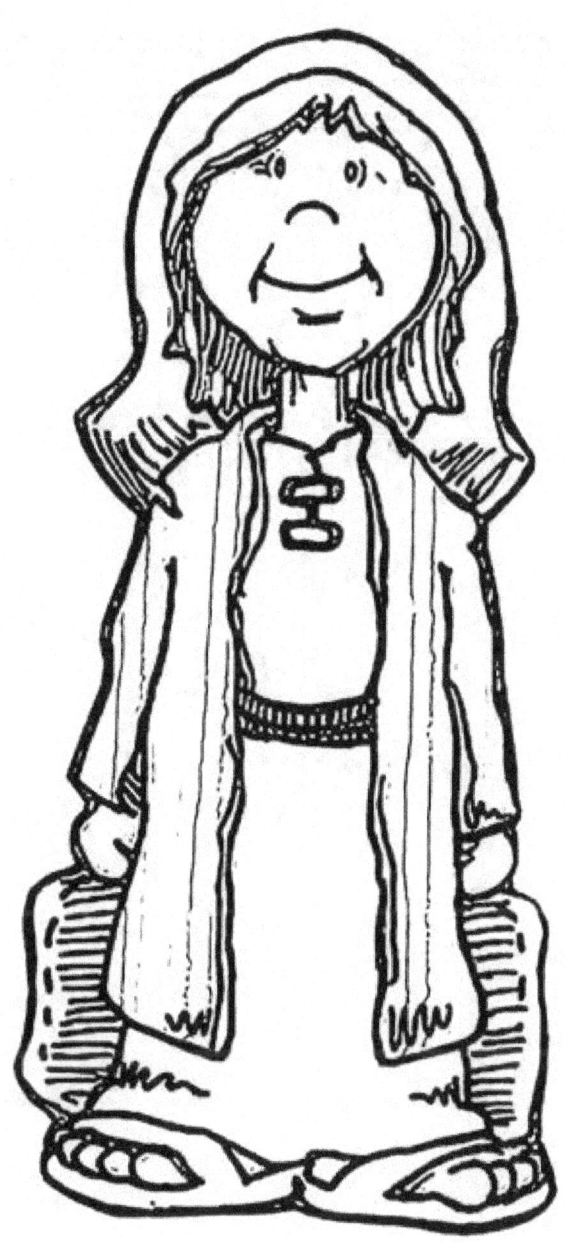

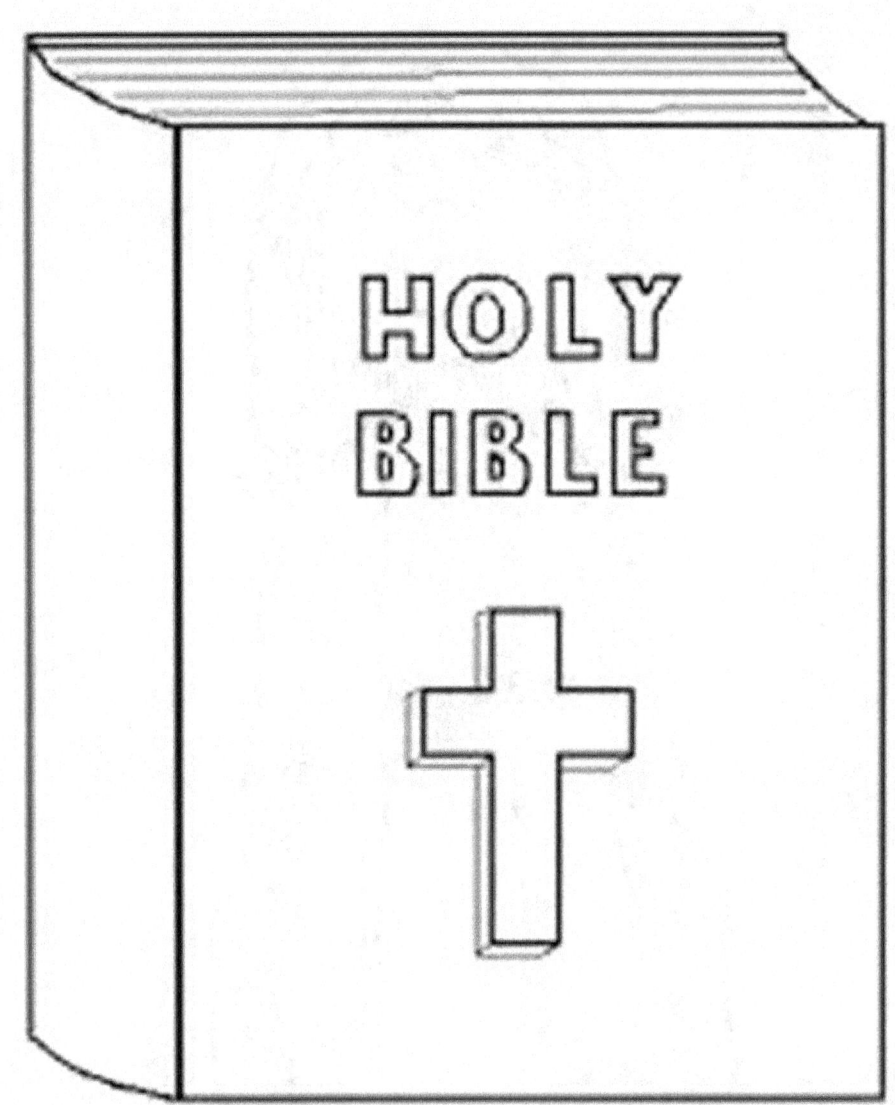

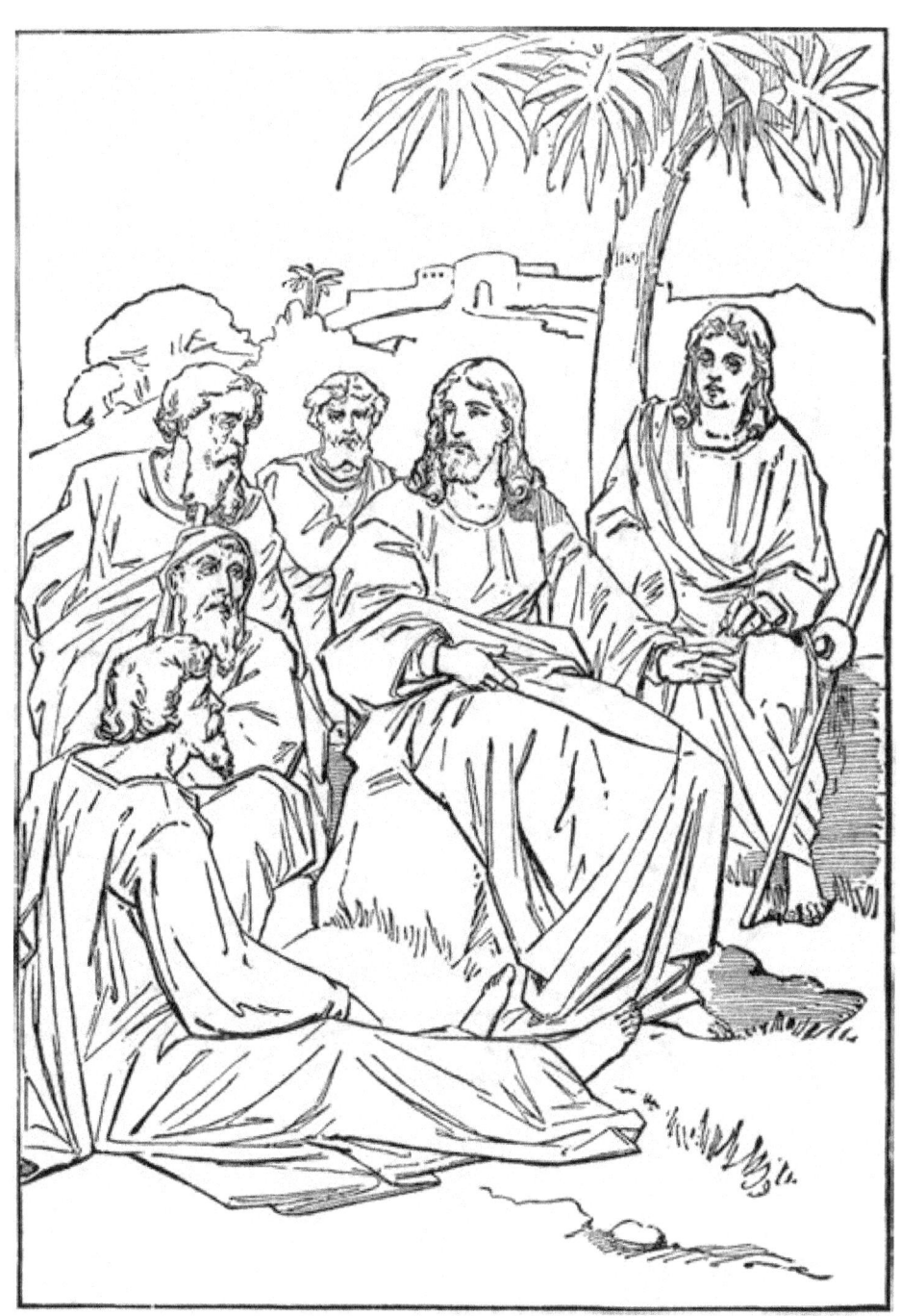

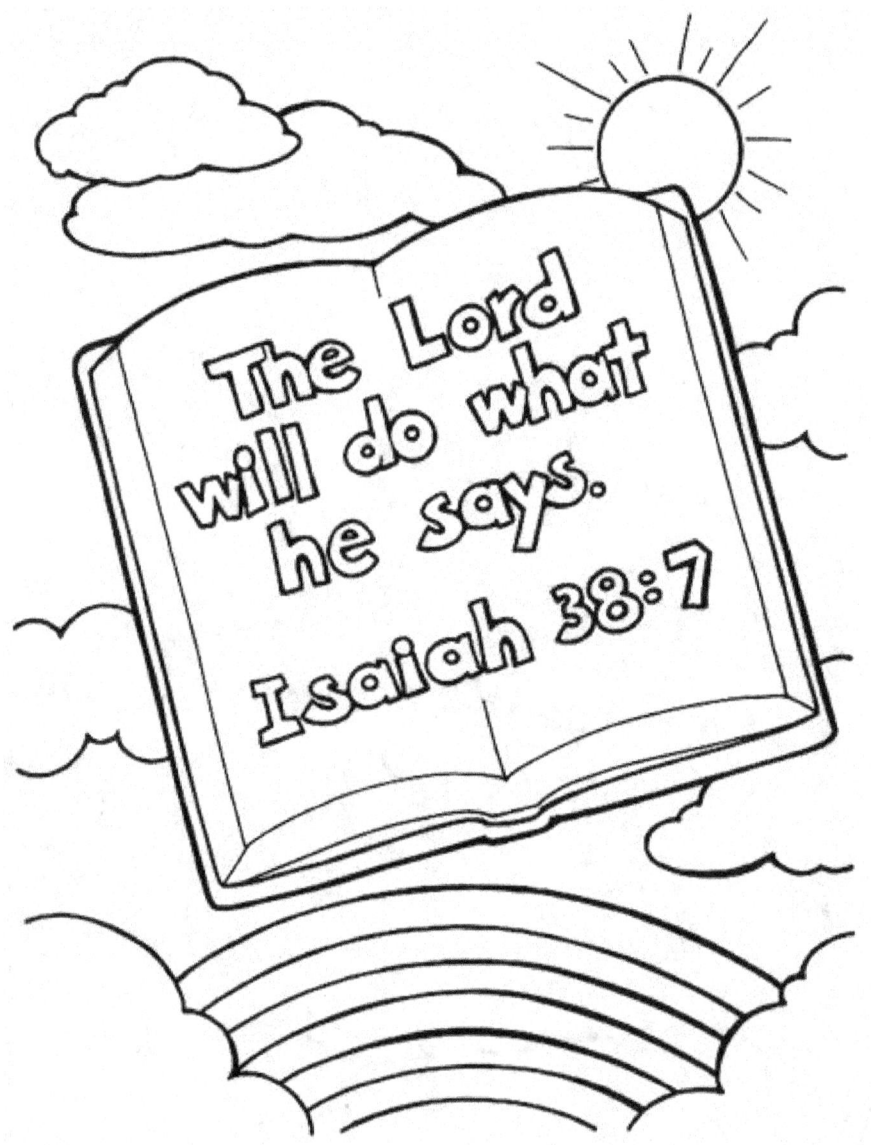

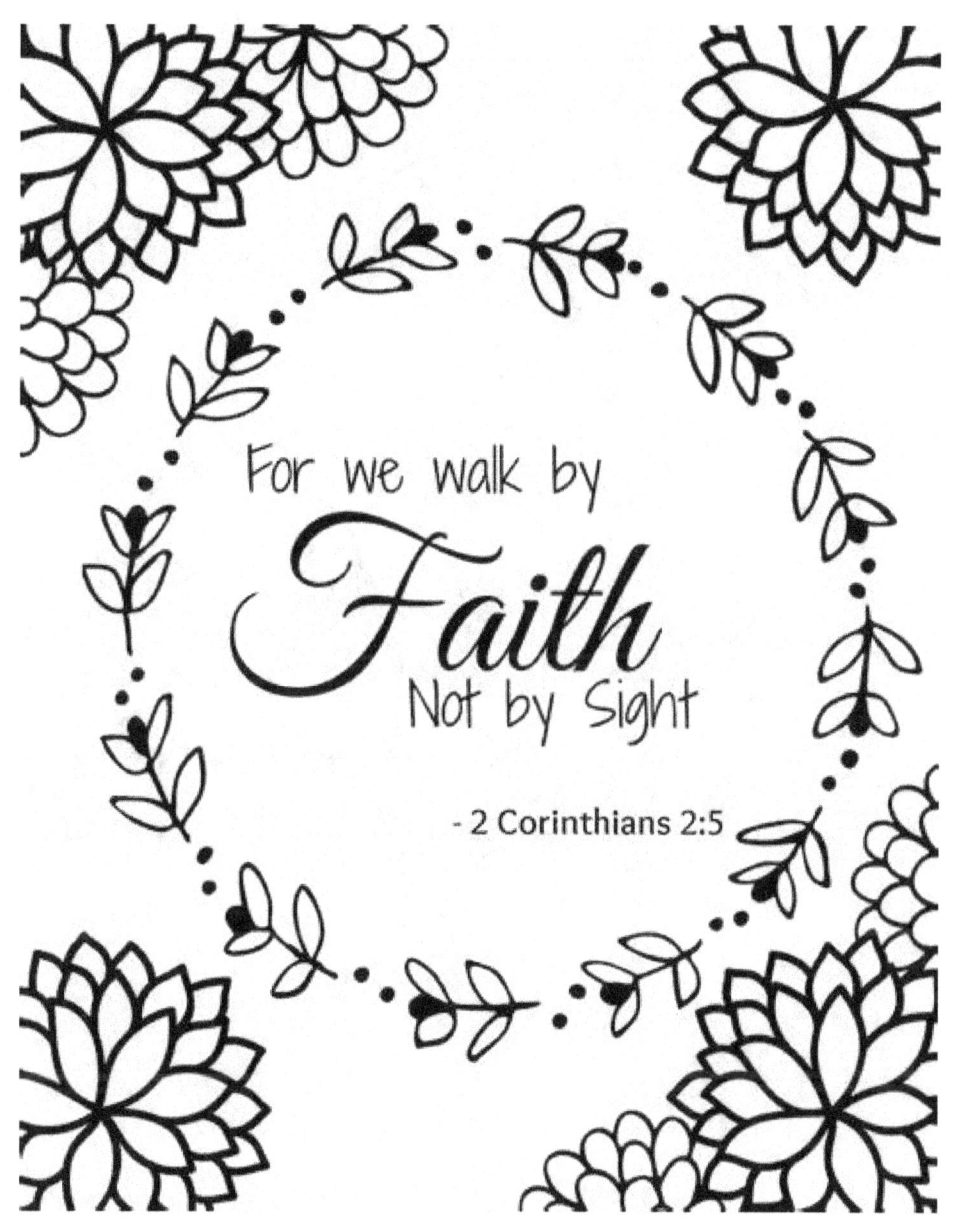

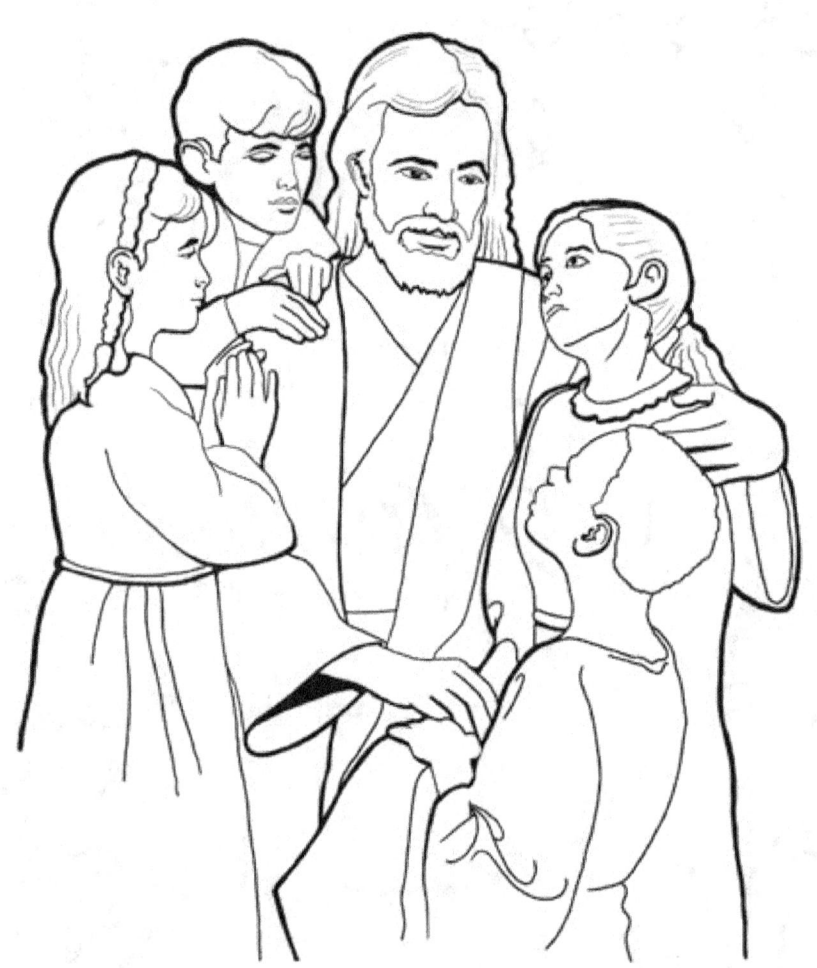

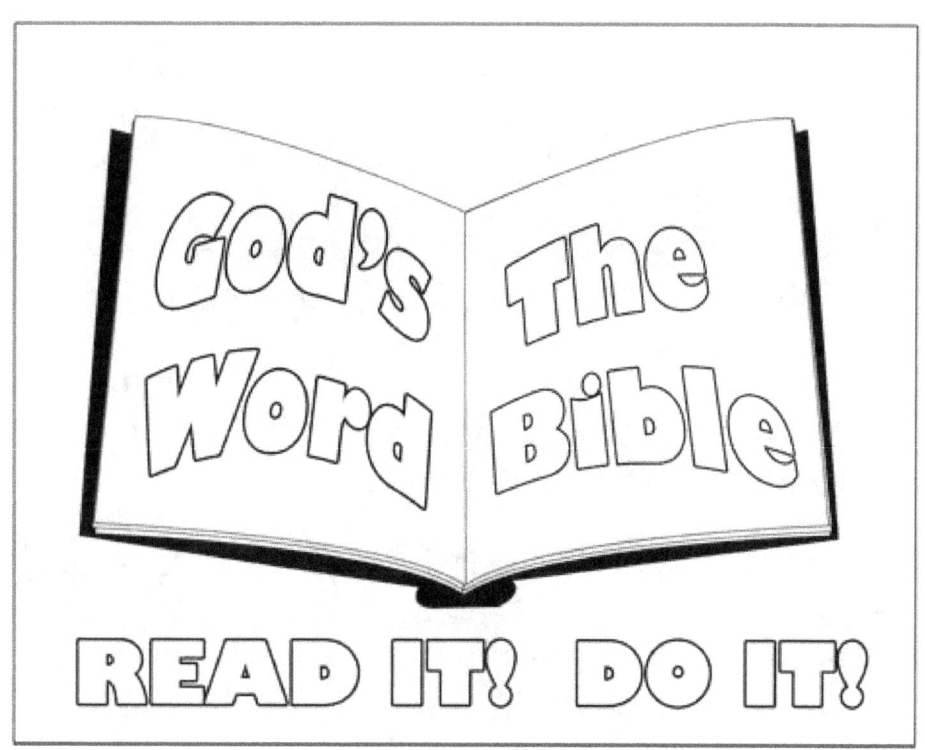

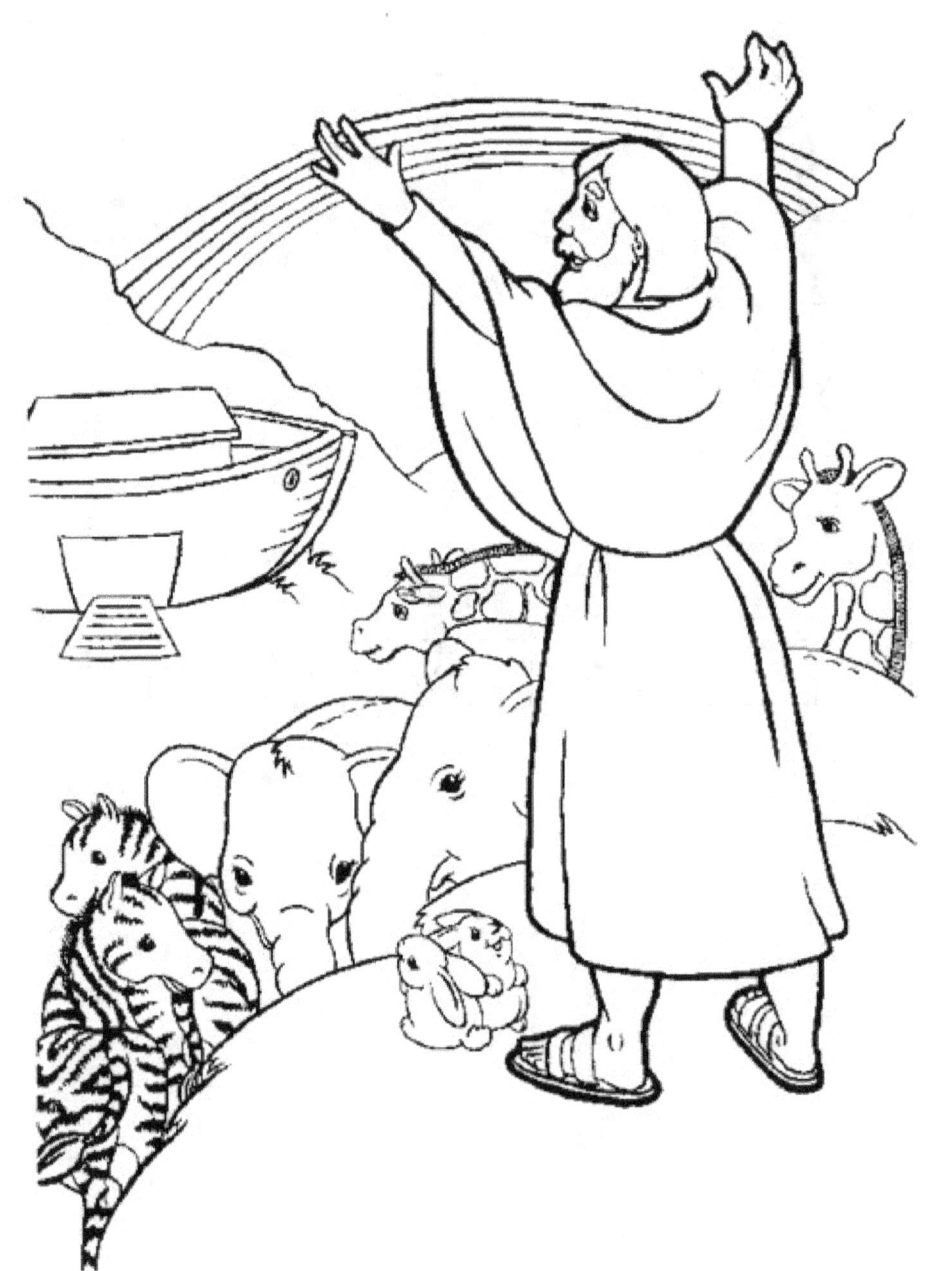

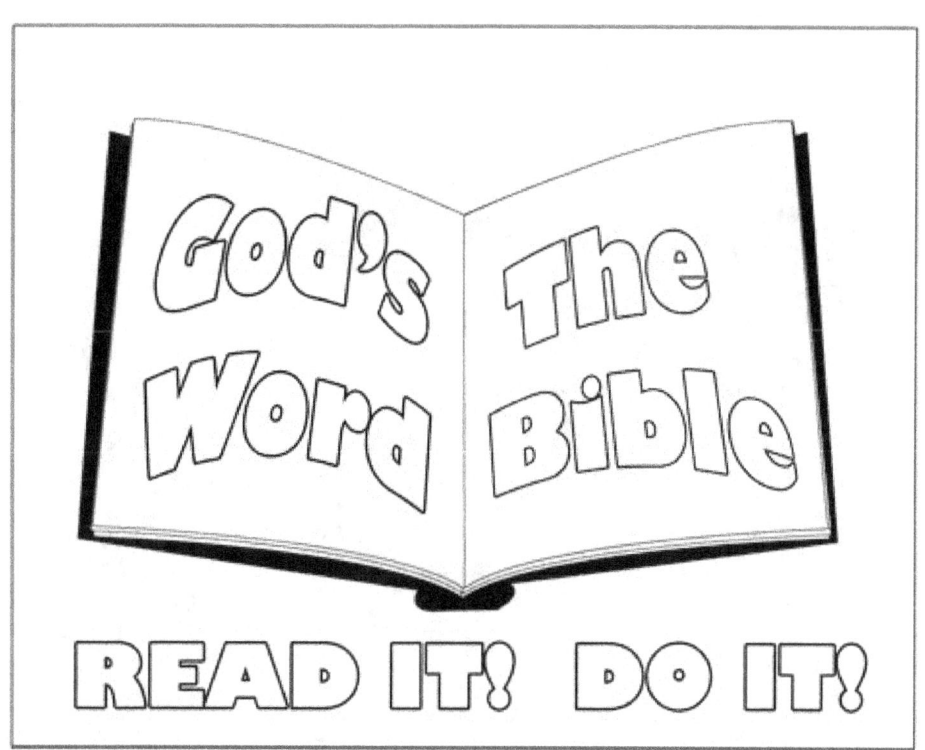

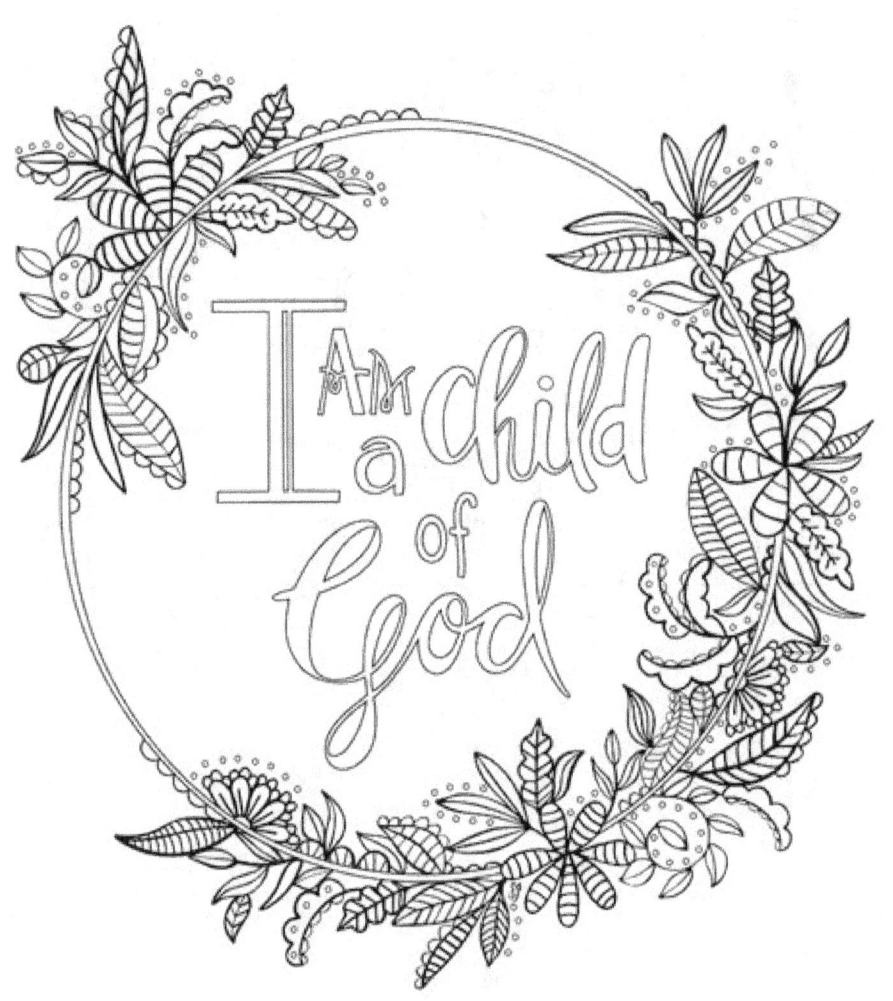

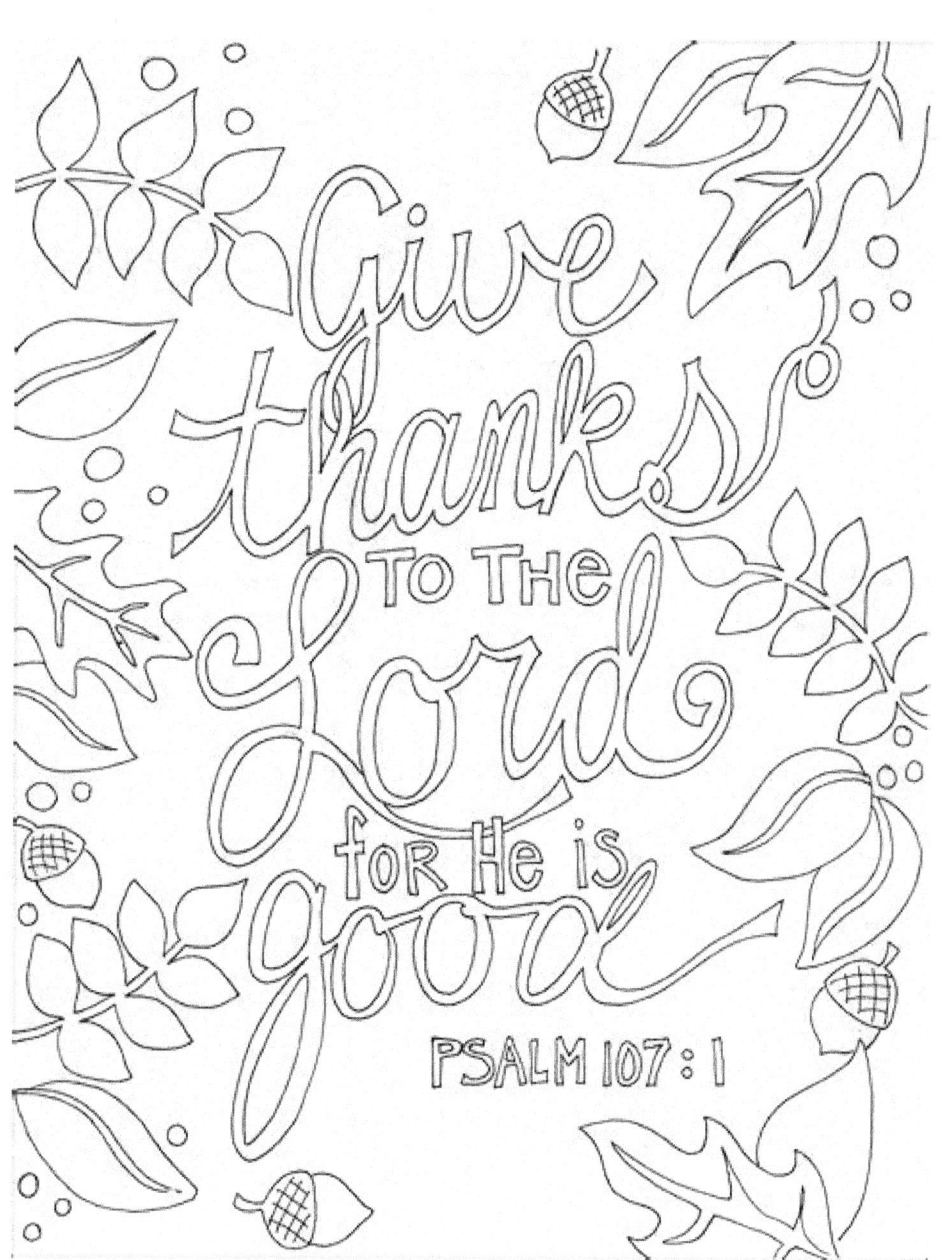

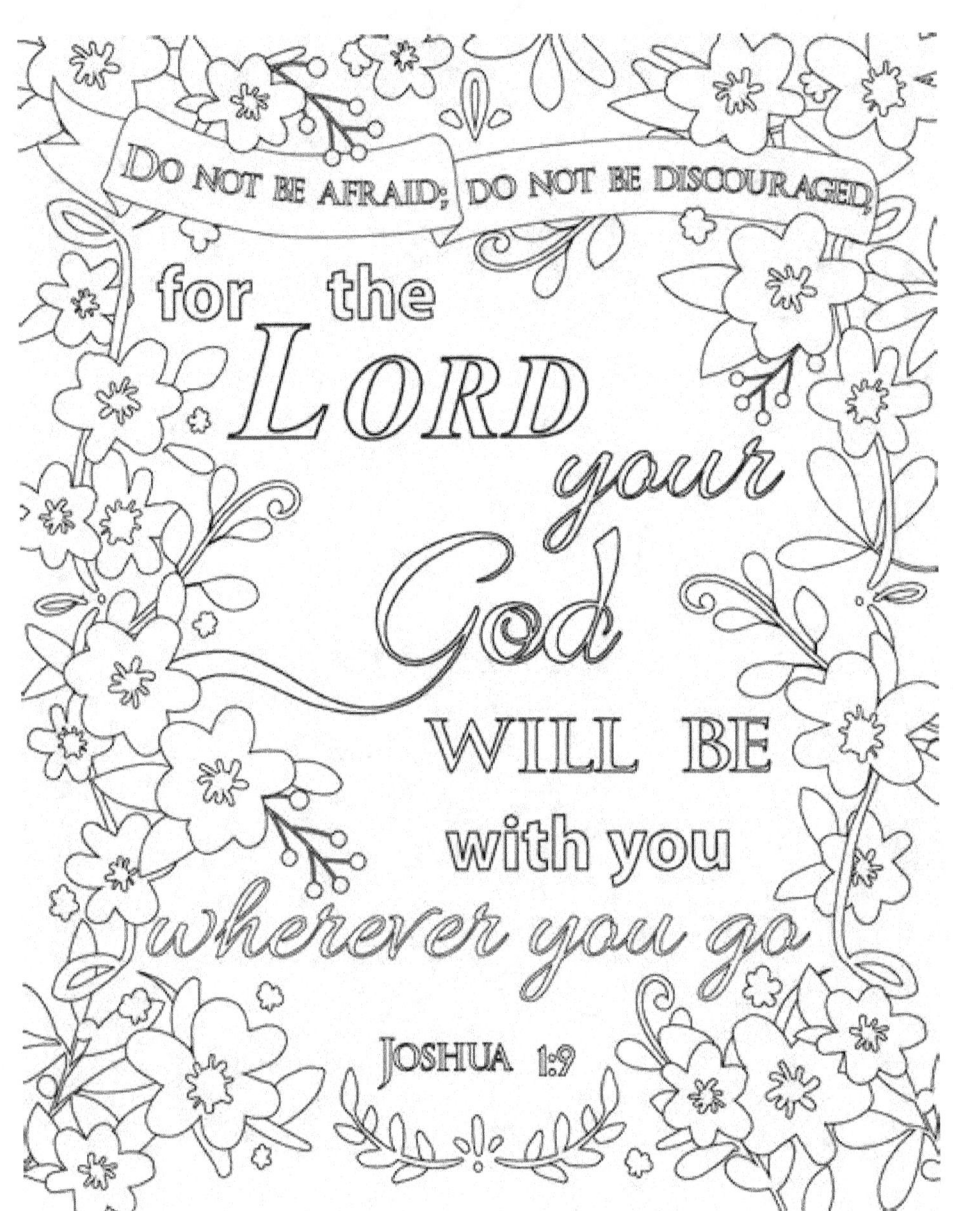

Do not be afraid; do not be discouraged for the *Lord* your *God* will be with you *wherever you go*

Joshua 1:9

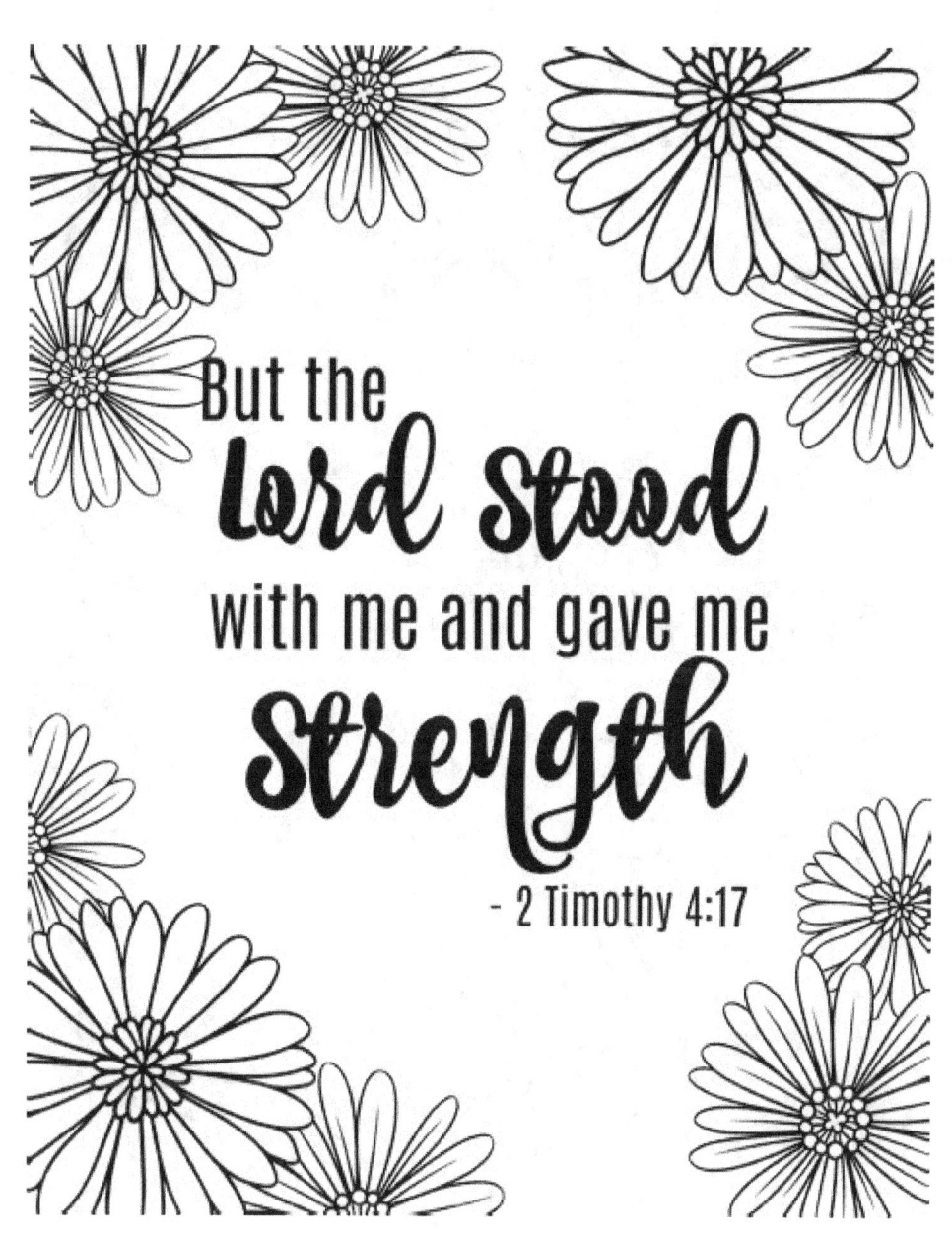

But the
Lord Stood
with me and gave me
Strength

— 2 Timothy 4:17

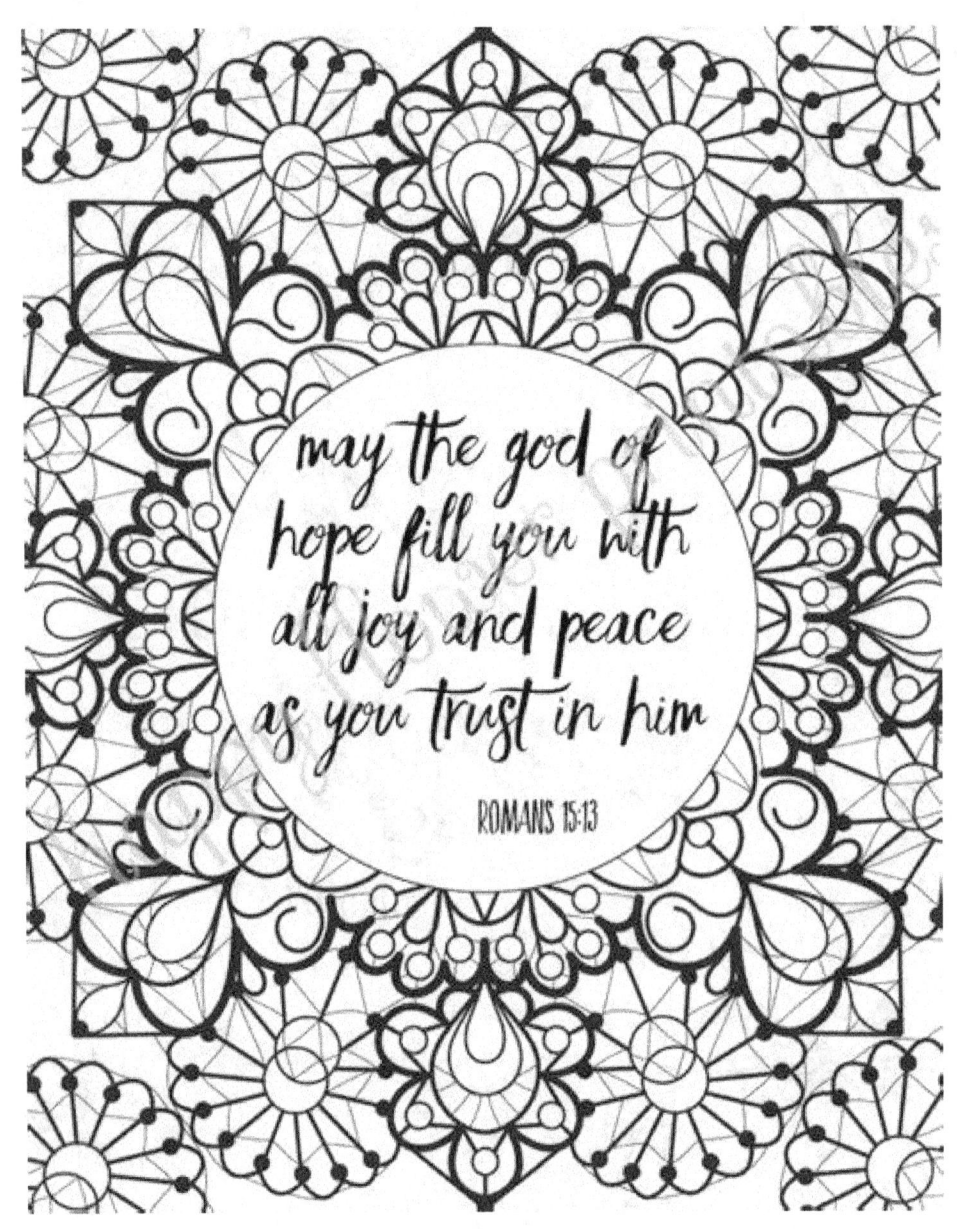

may the god of
hope fill you with
all joy and peace
as you trust in him

ROMANS 15:13

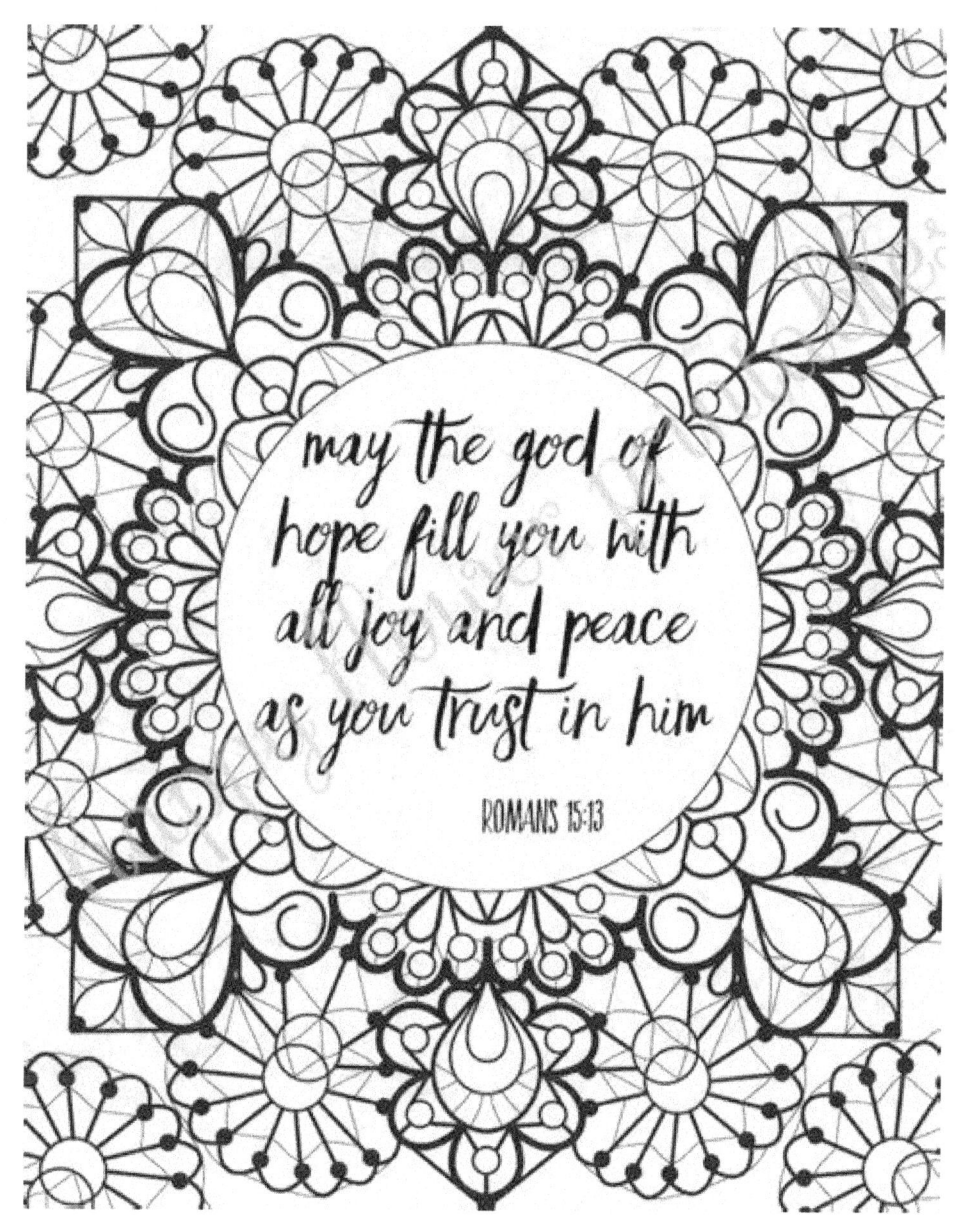

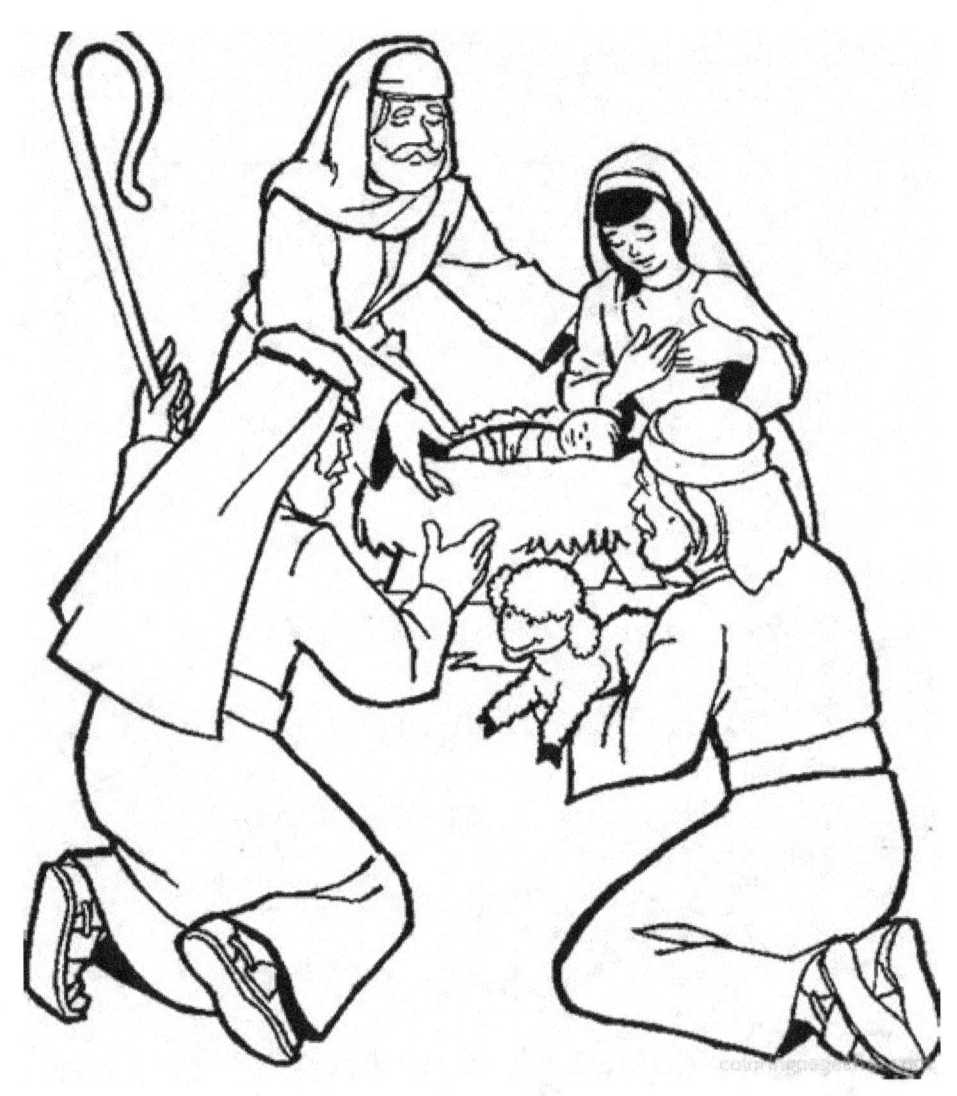

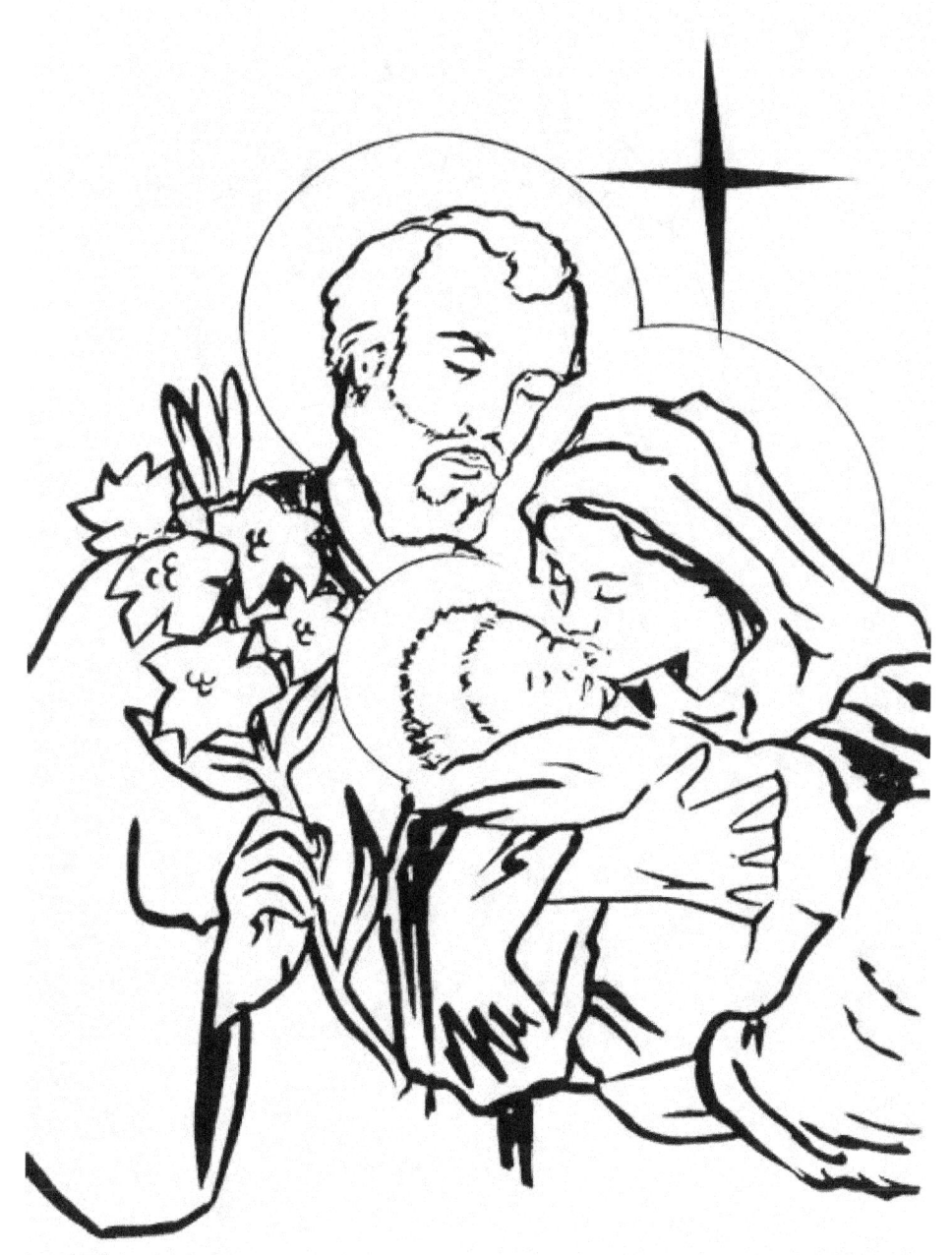

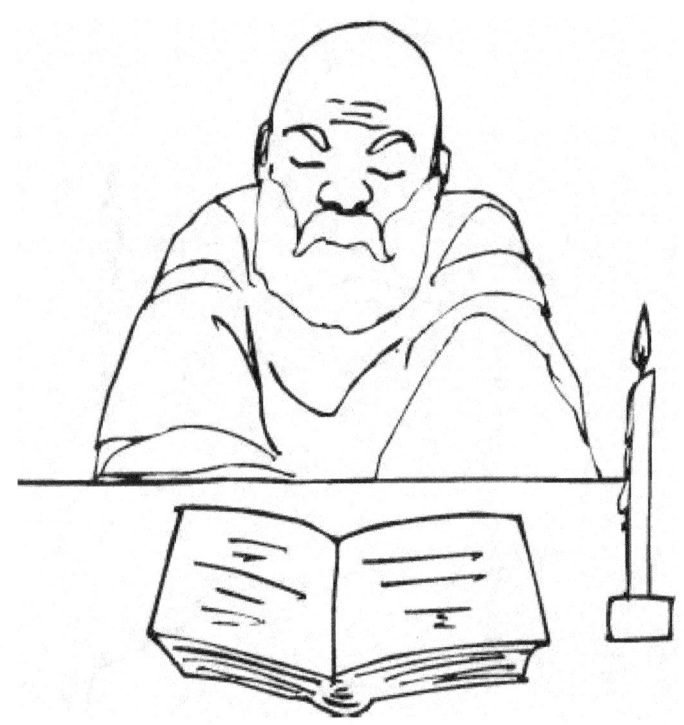

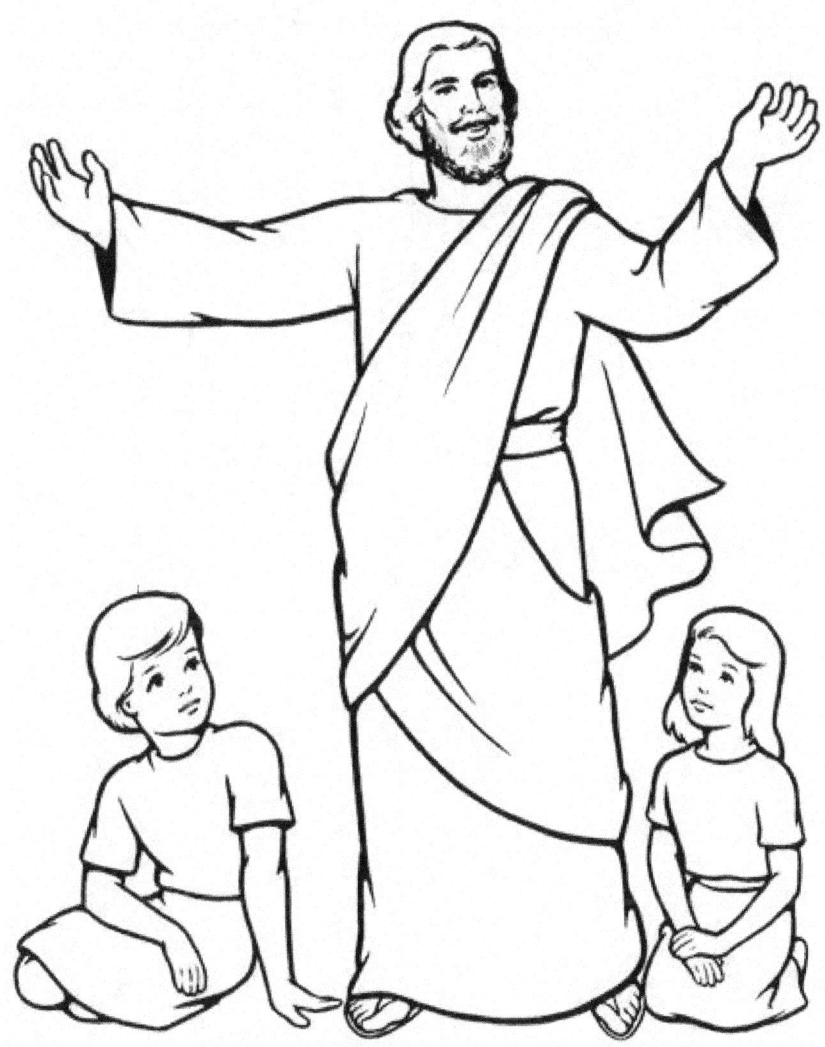

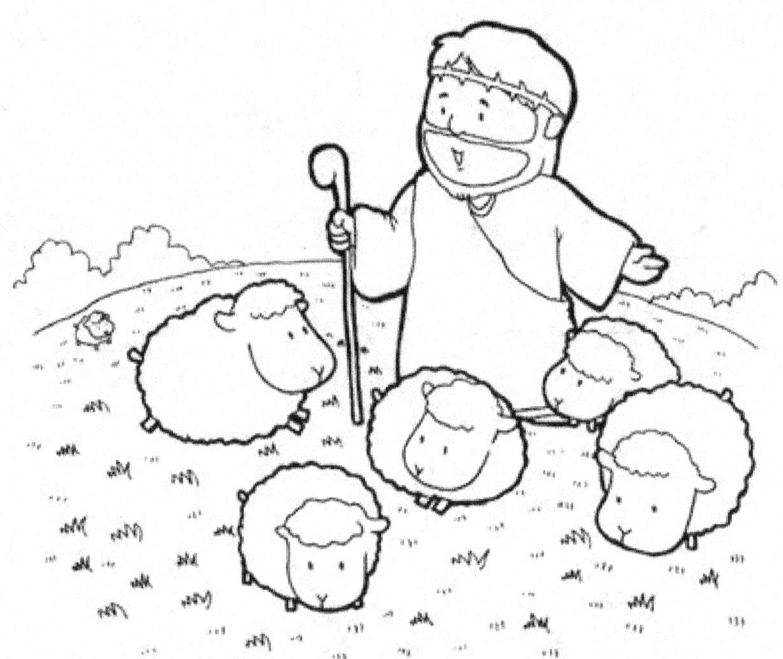

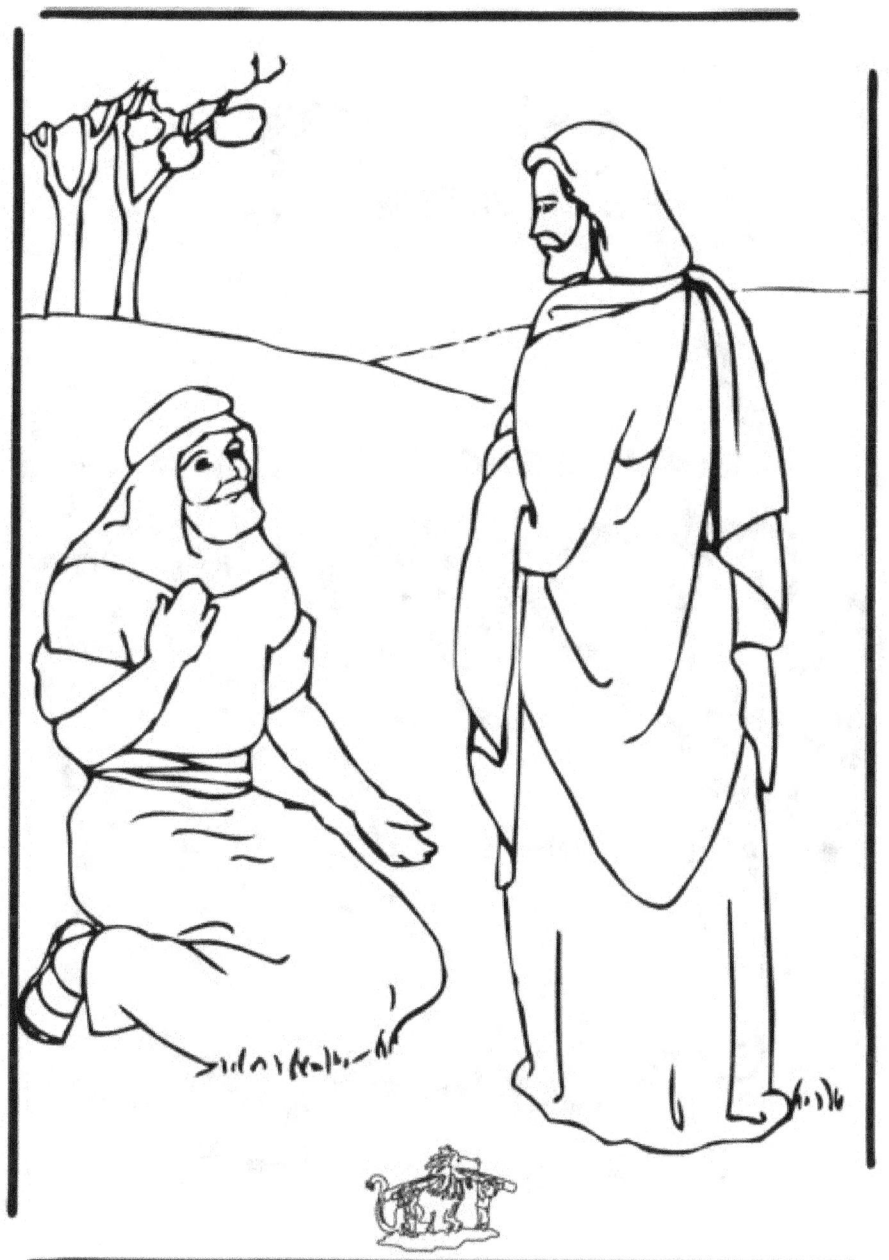

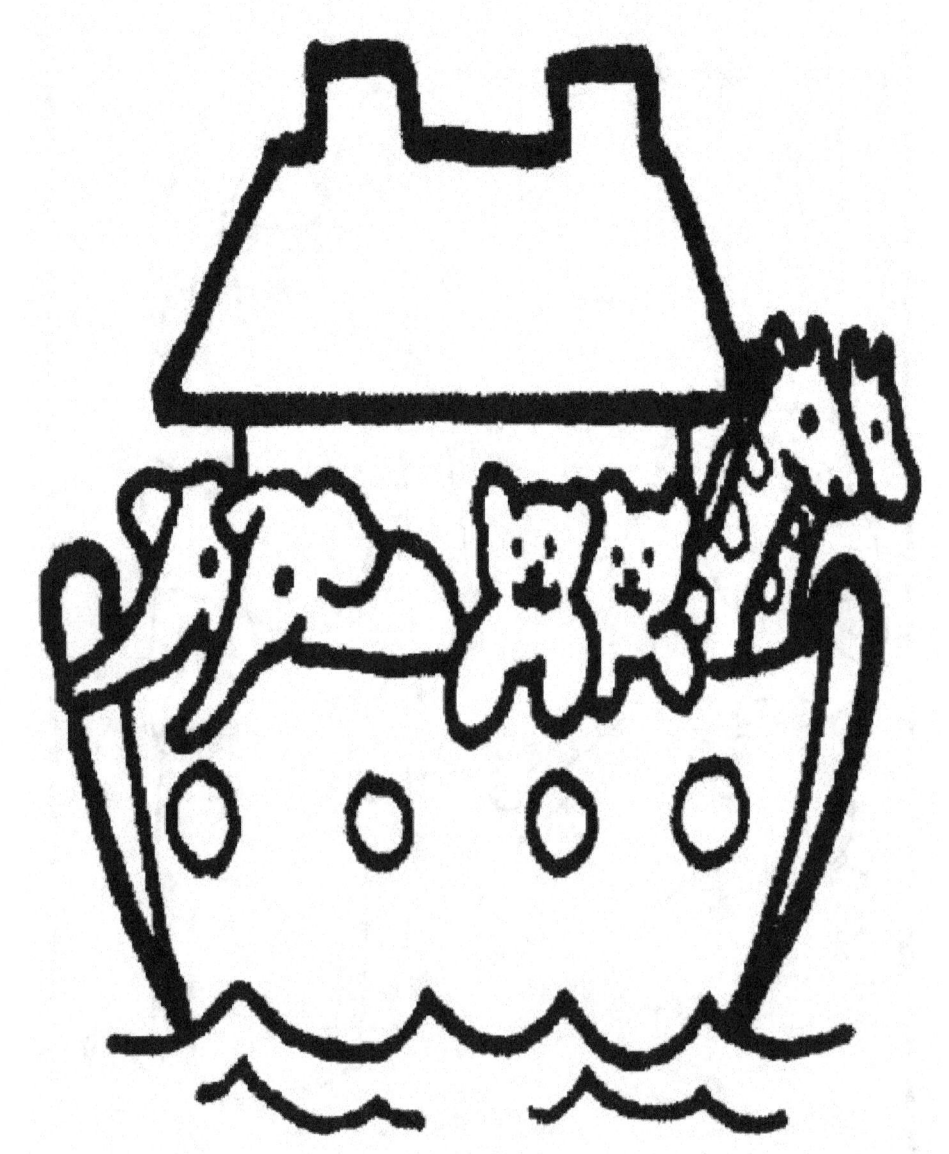

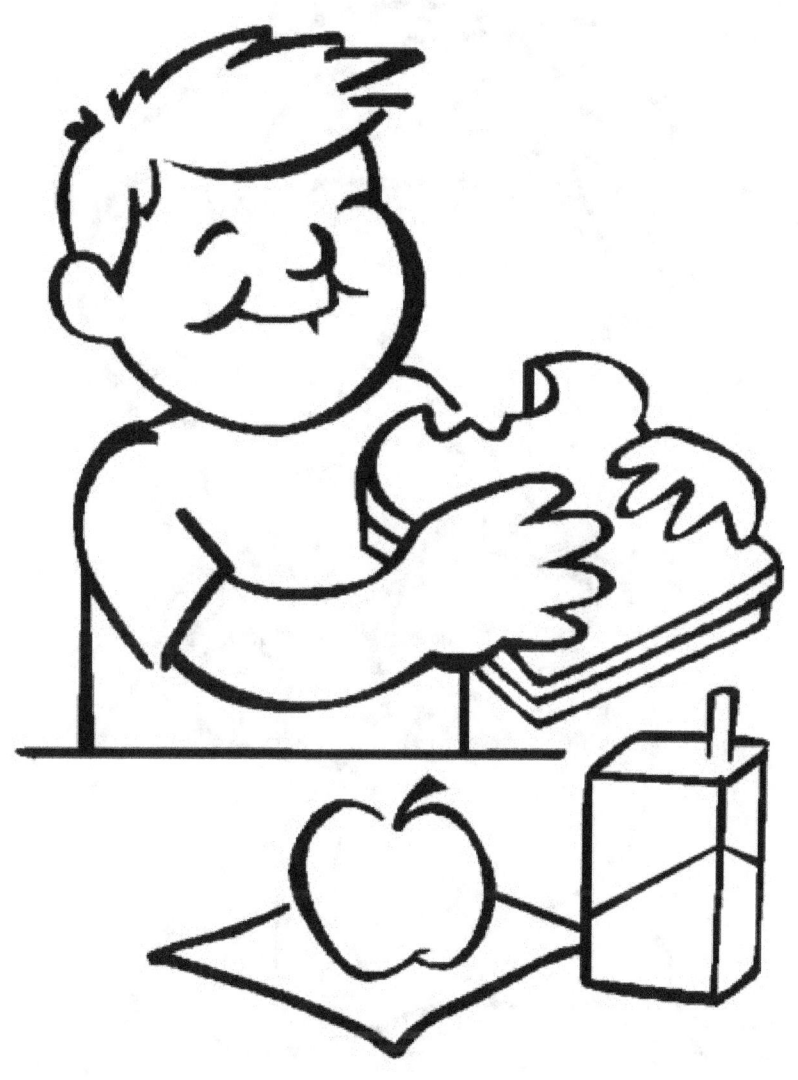

Give us this day our daily bread;

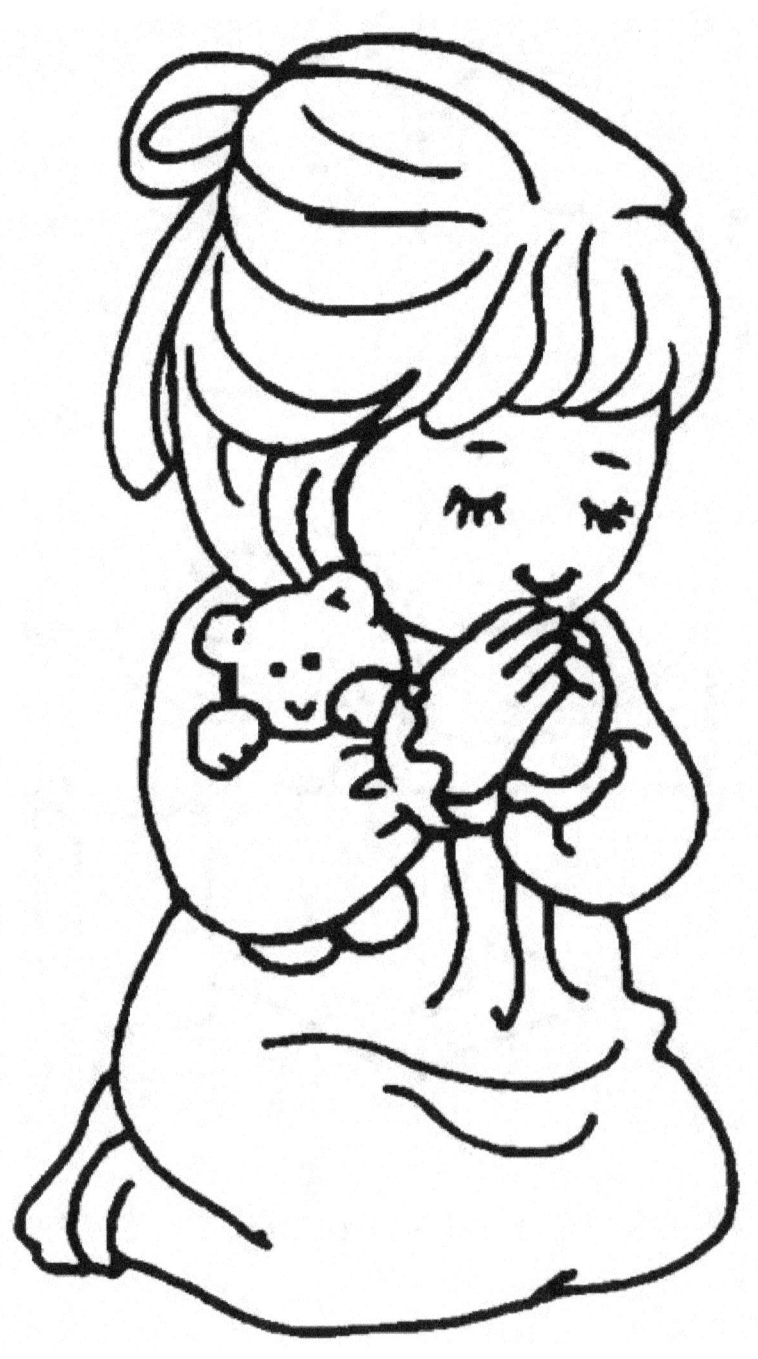

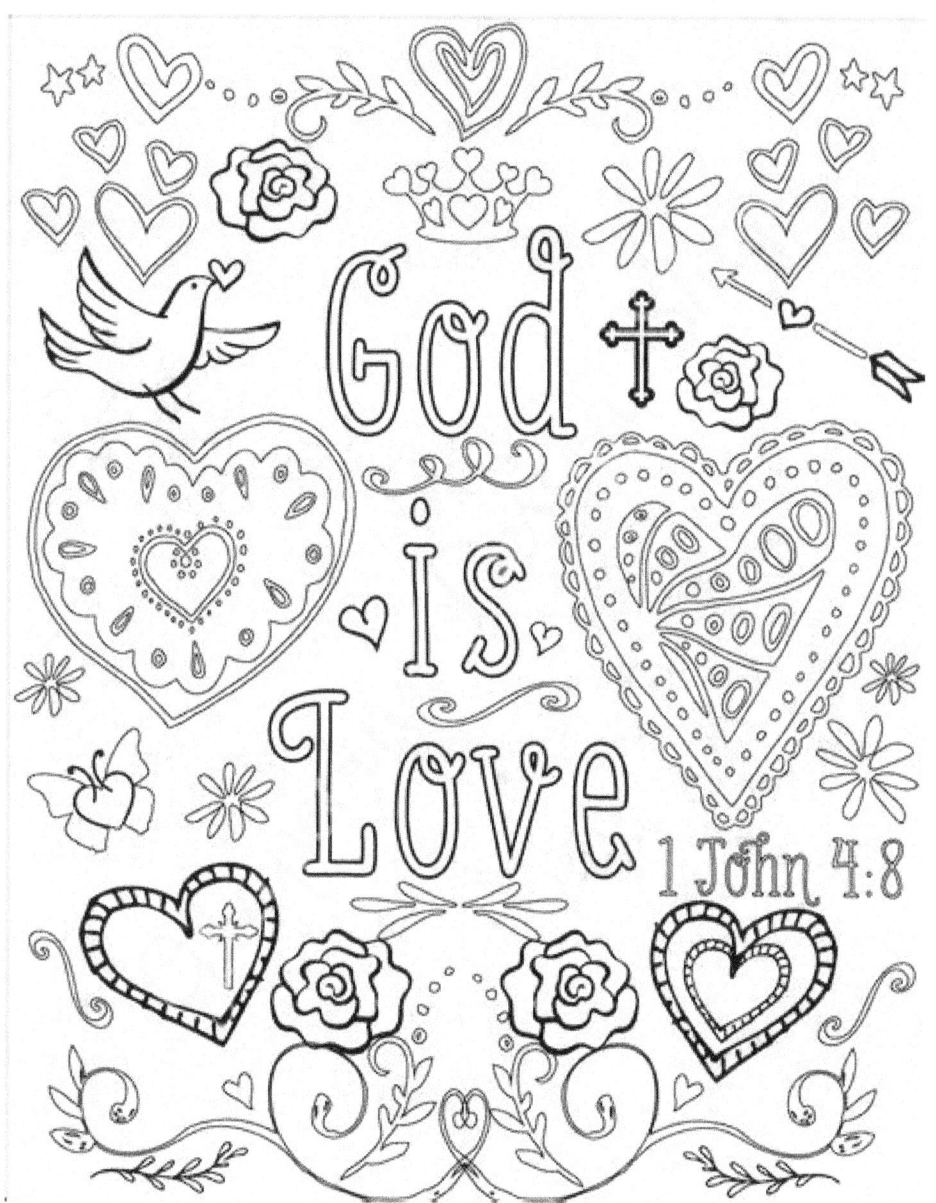

God is Love

1 John 4:8

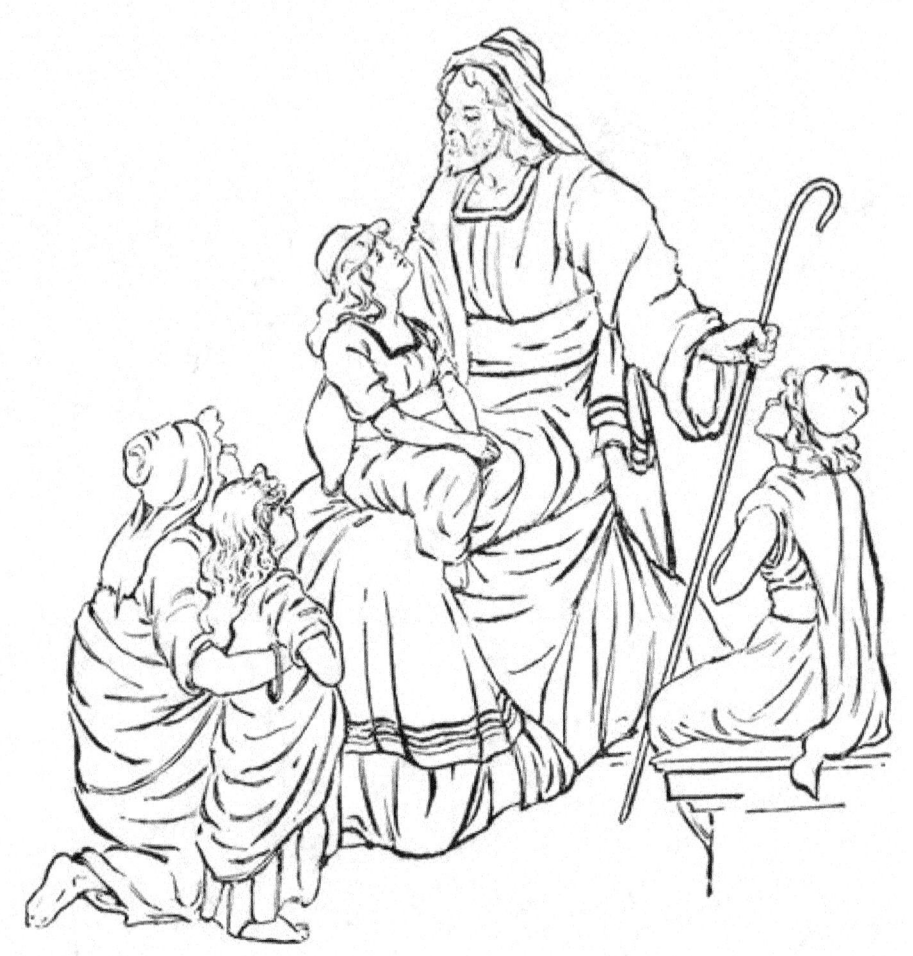

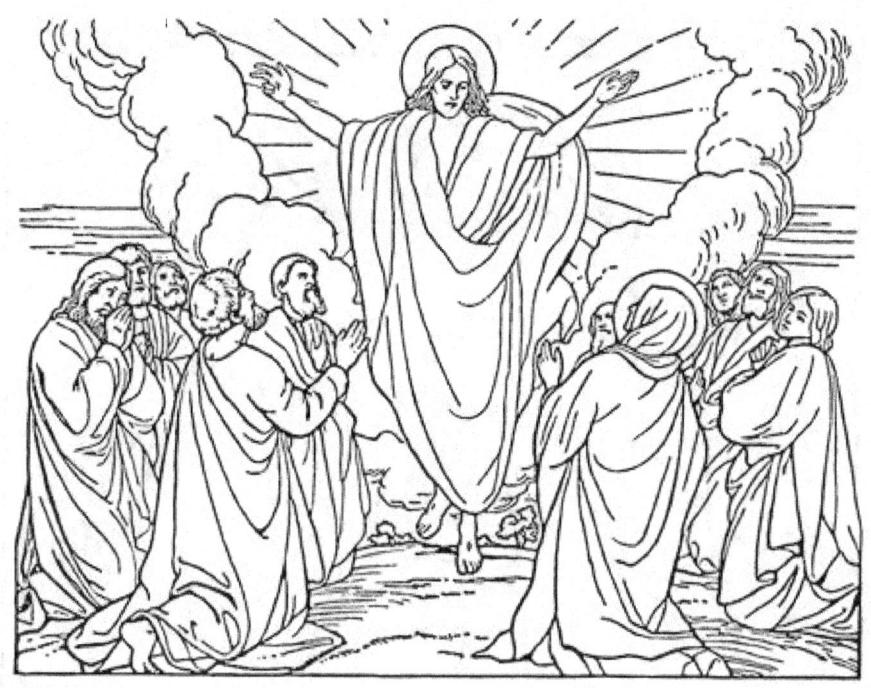

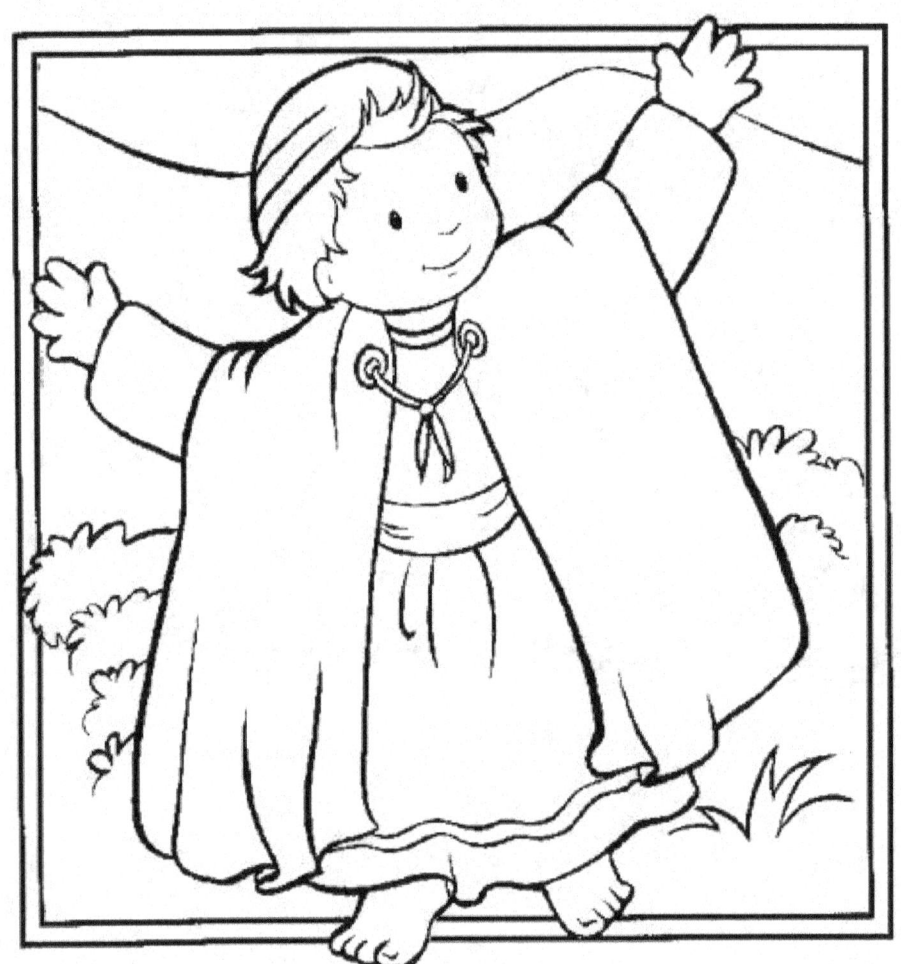

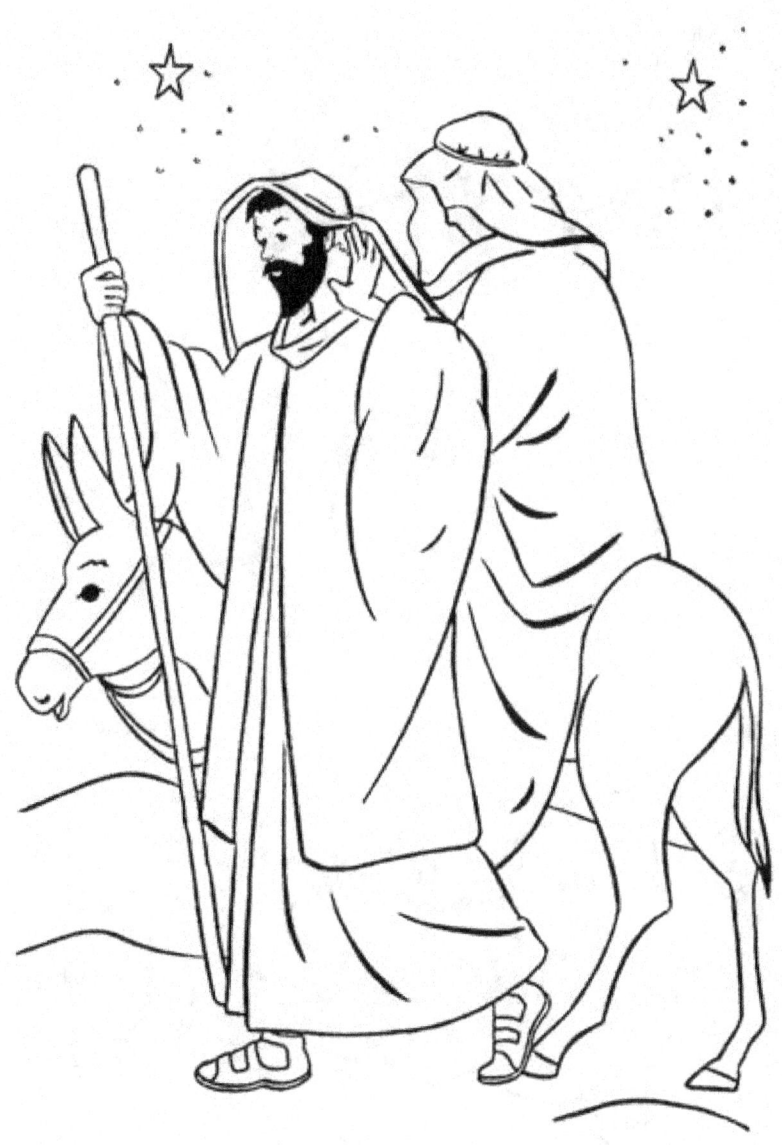

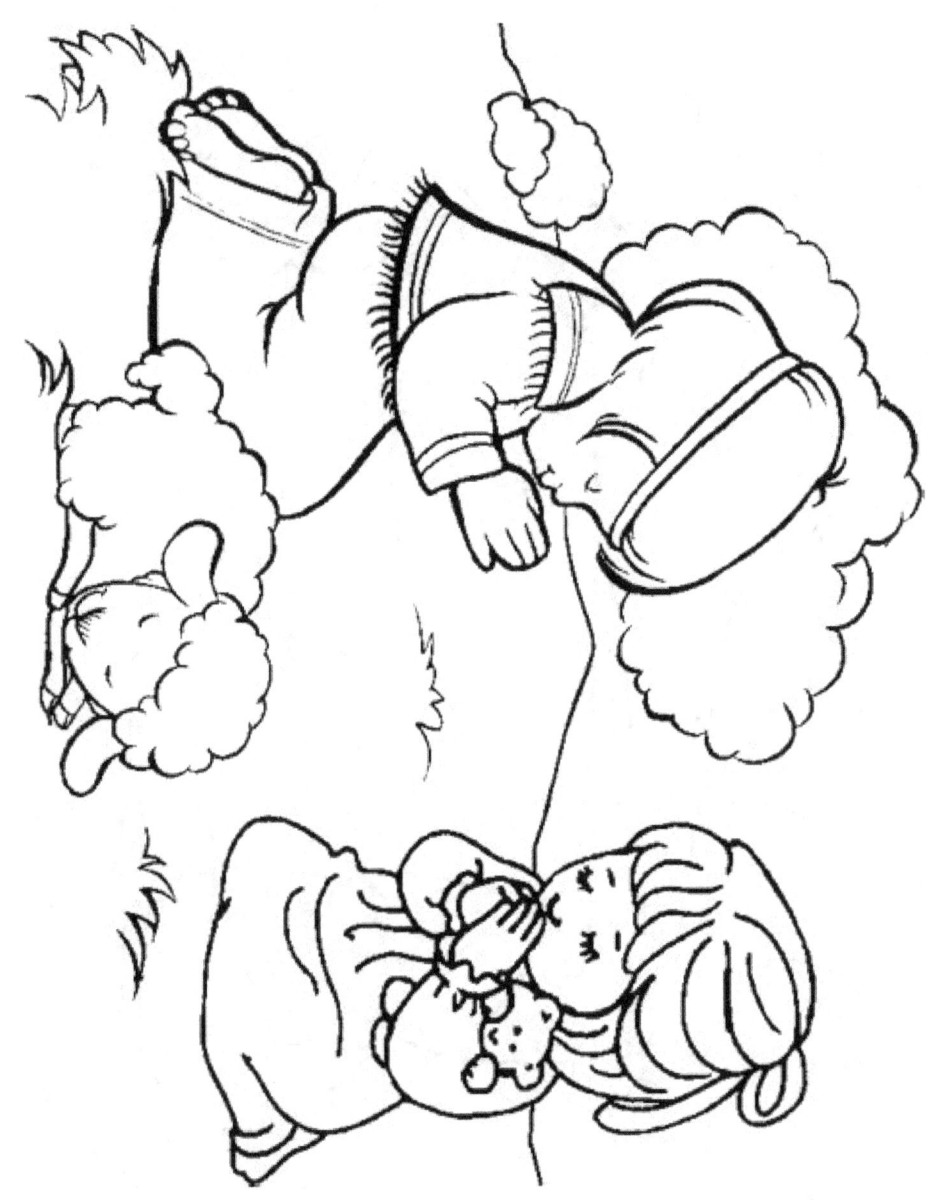

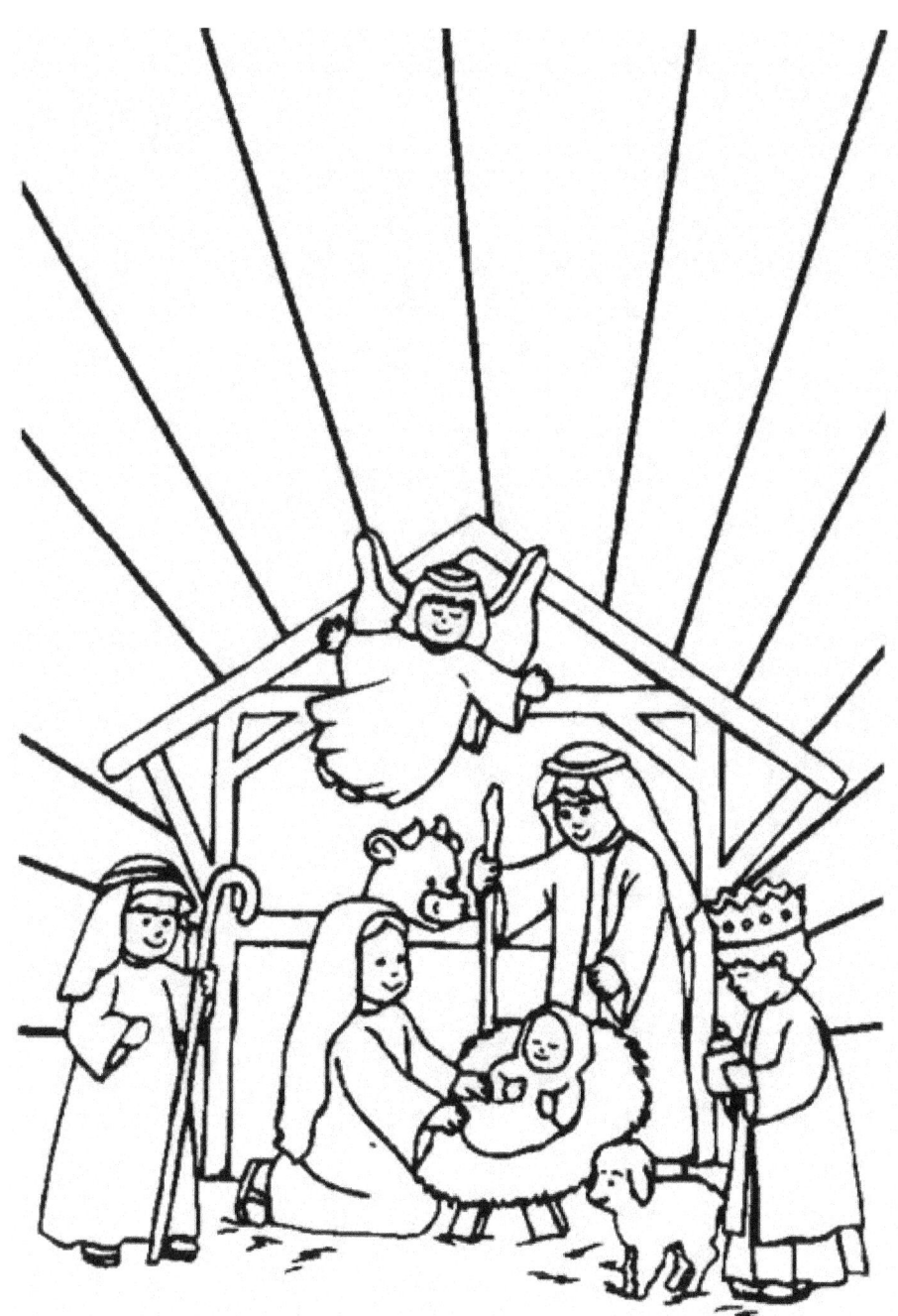

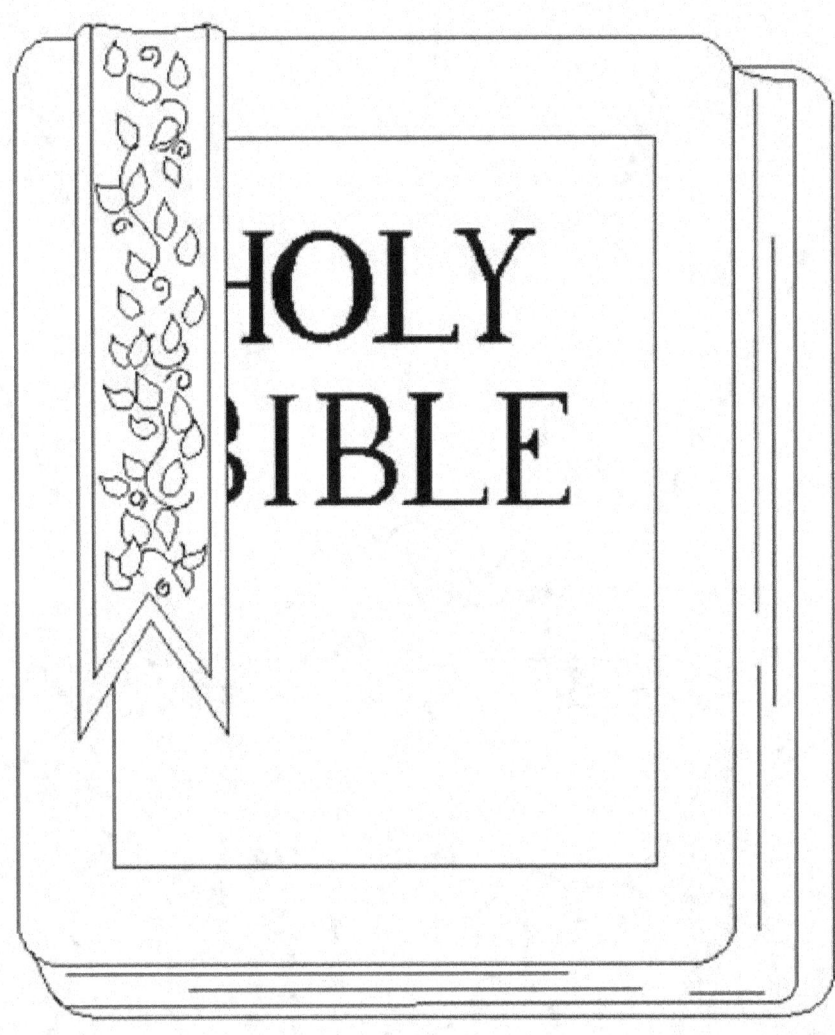

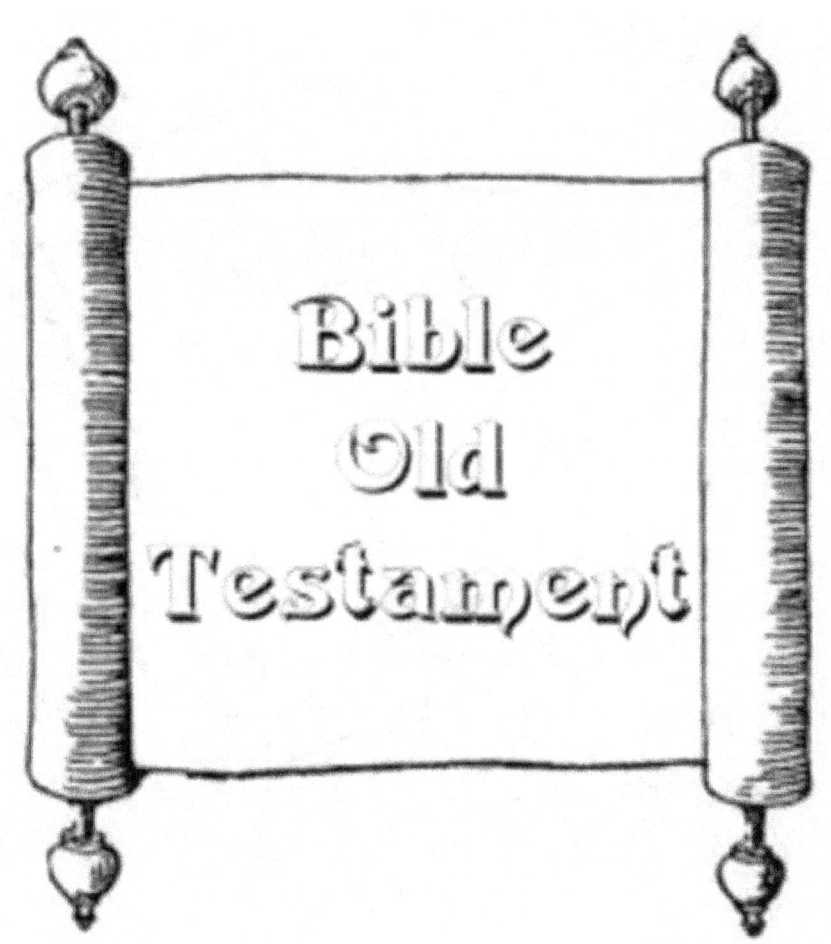

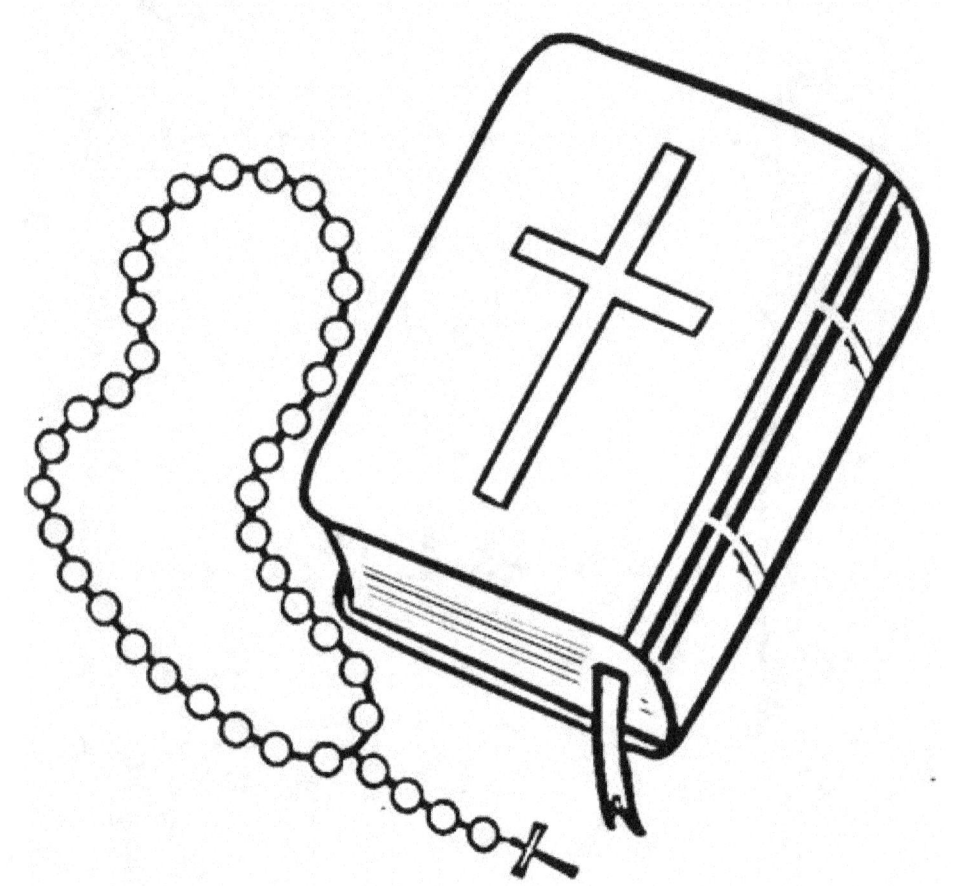

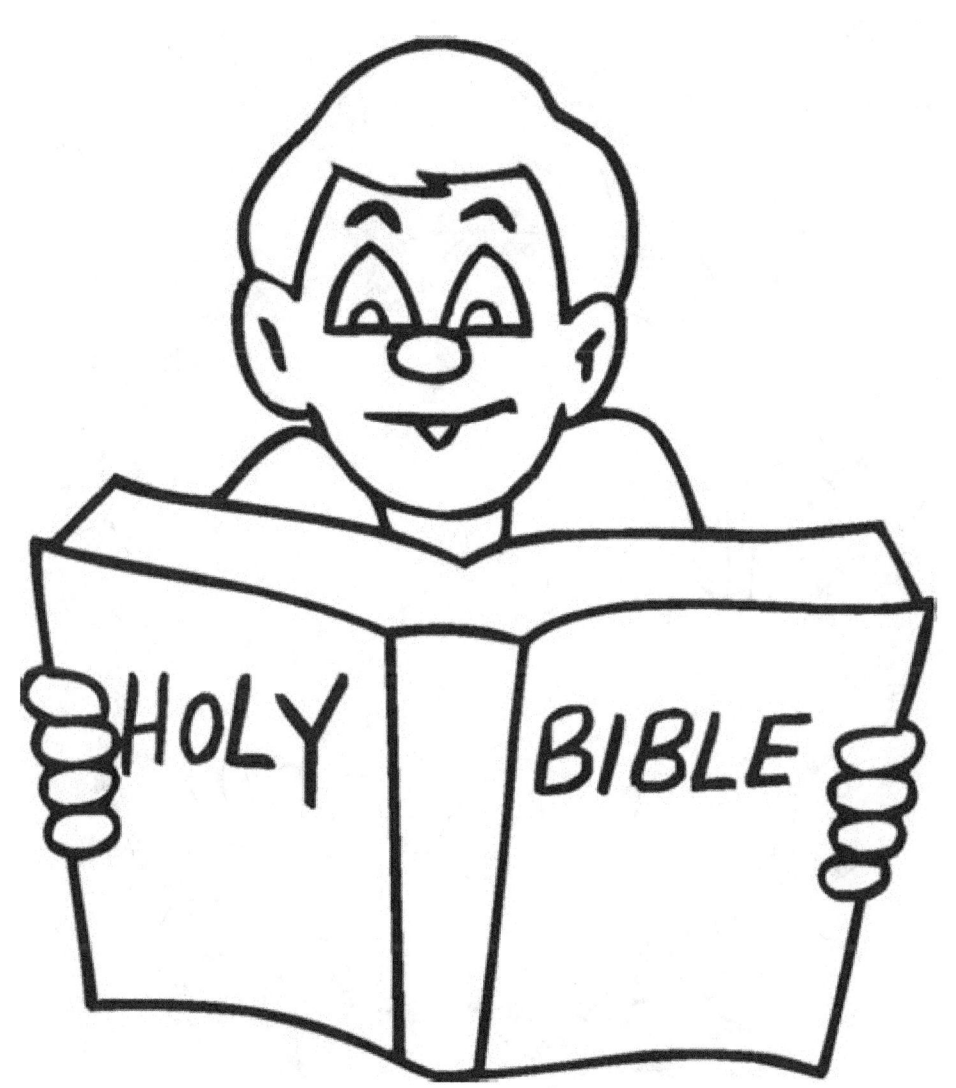

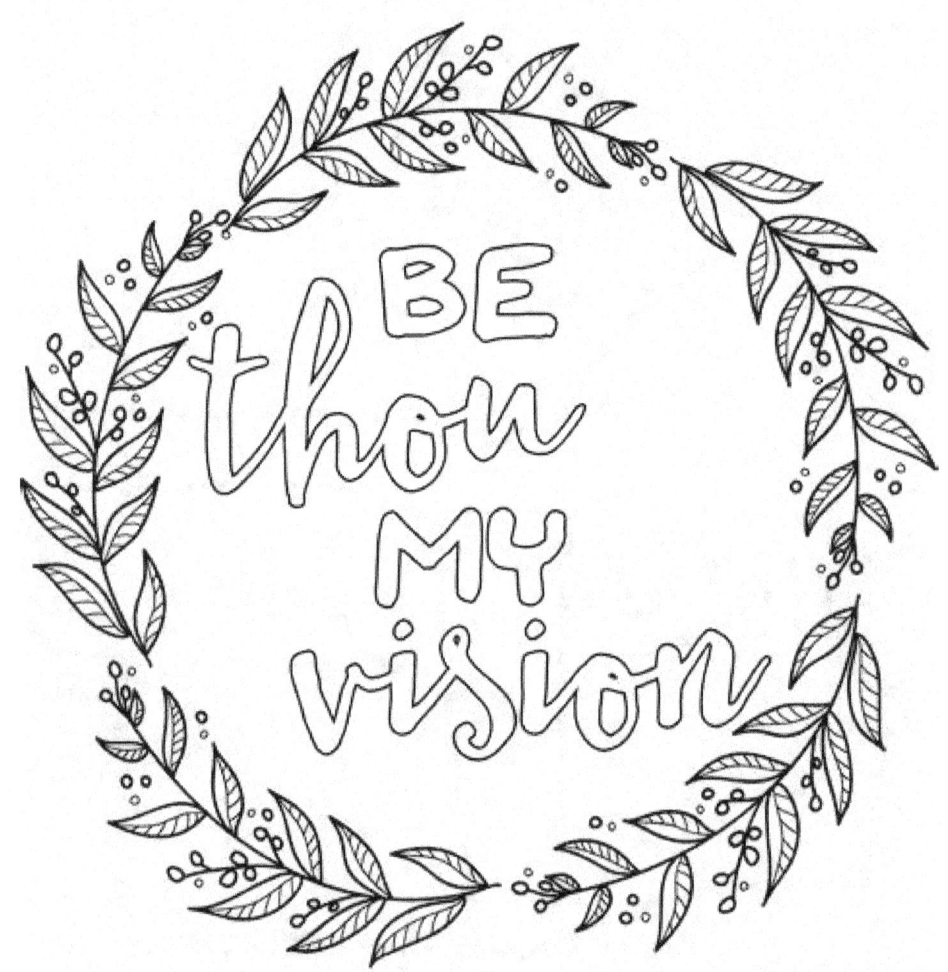

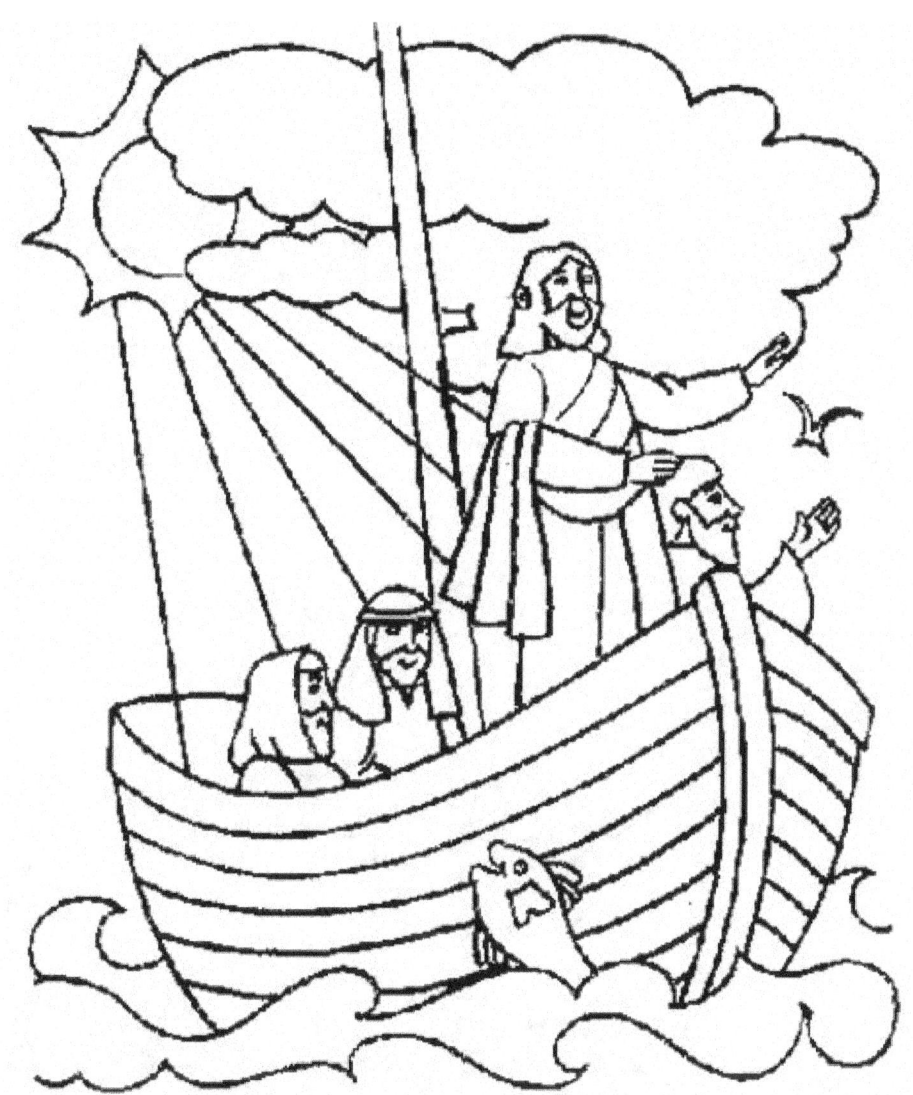

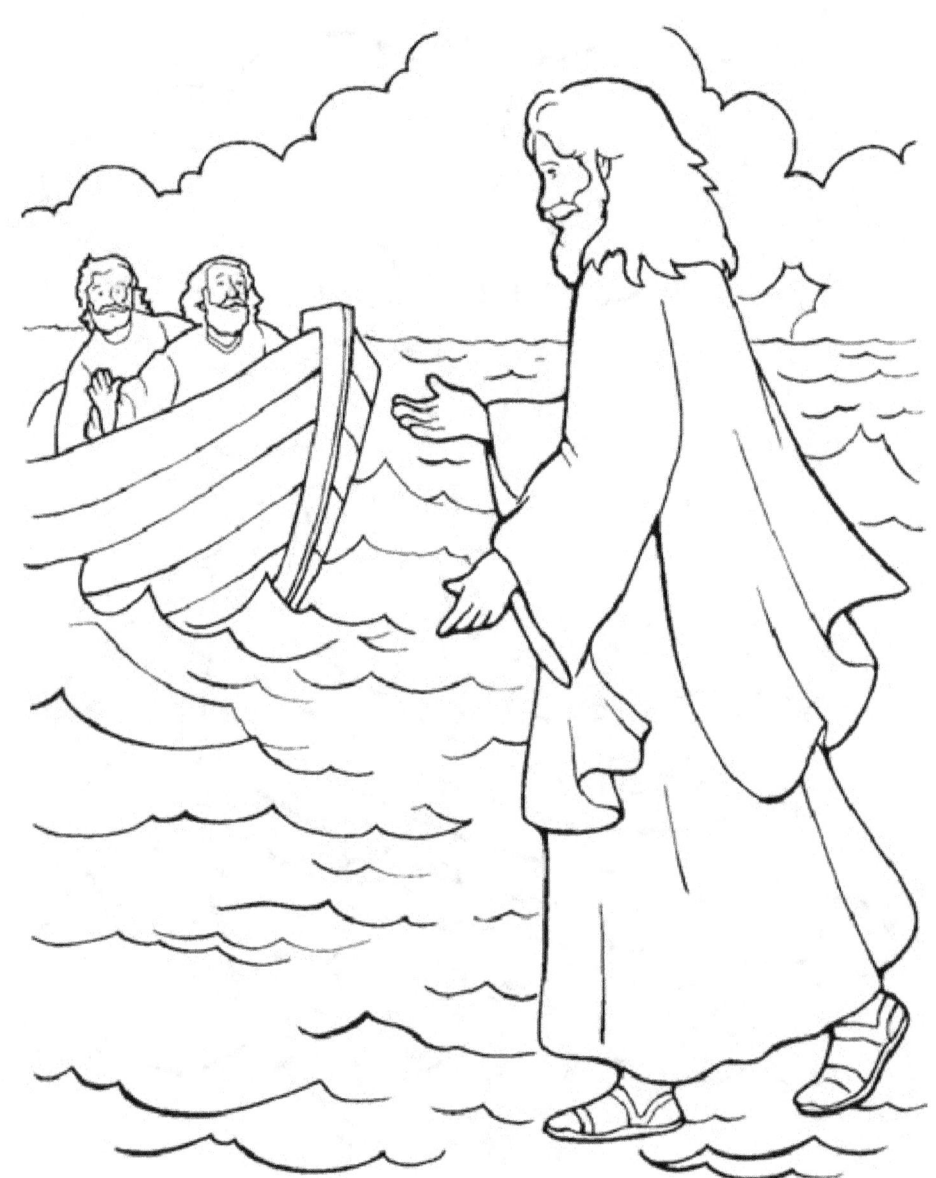

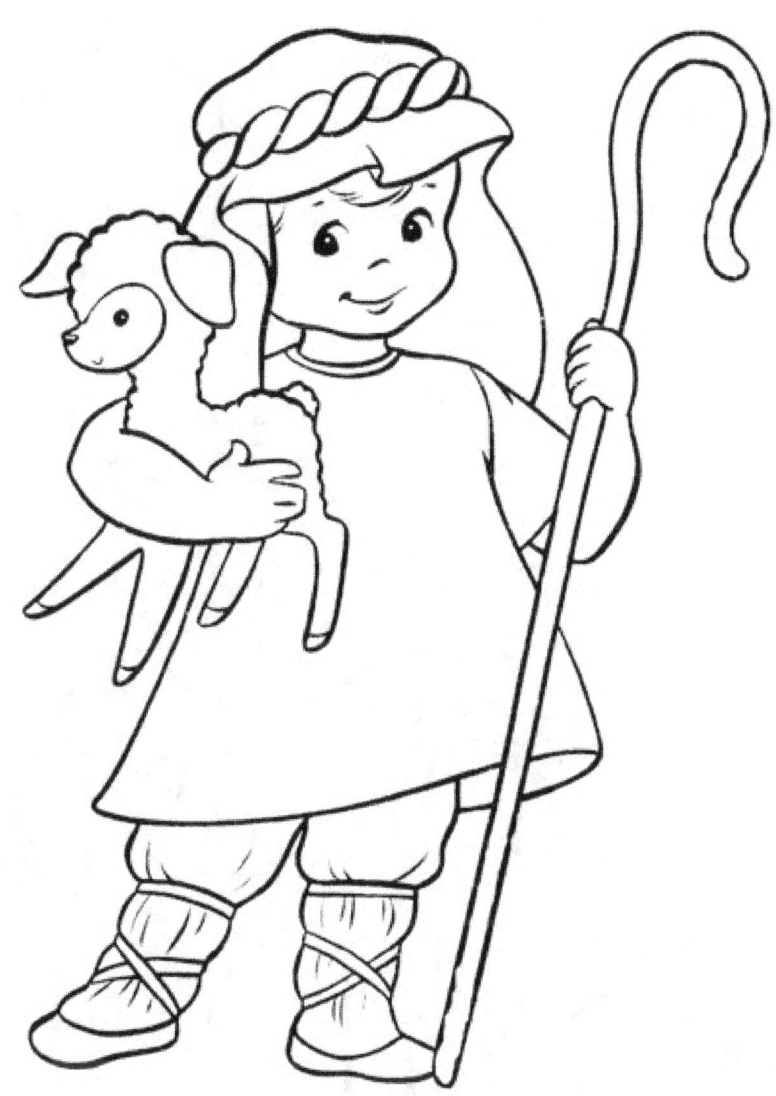

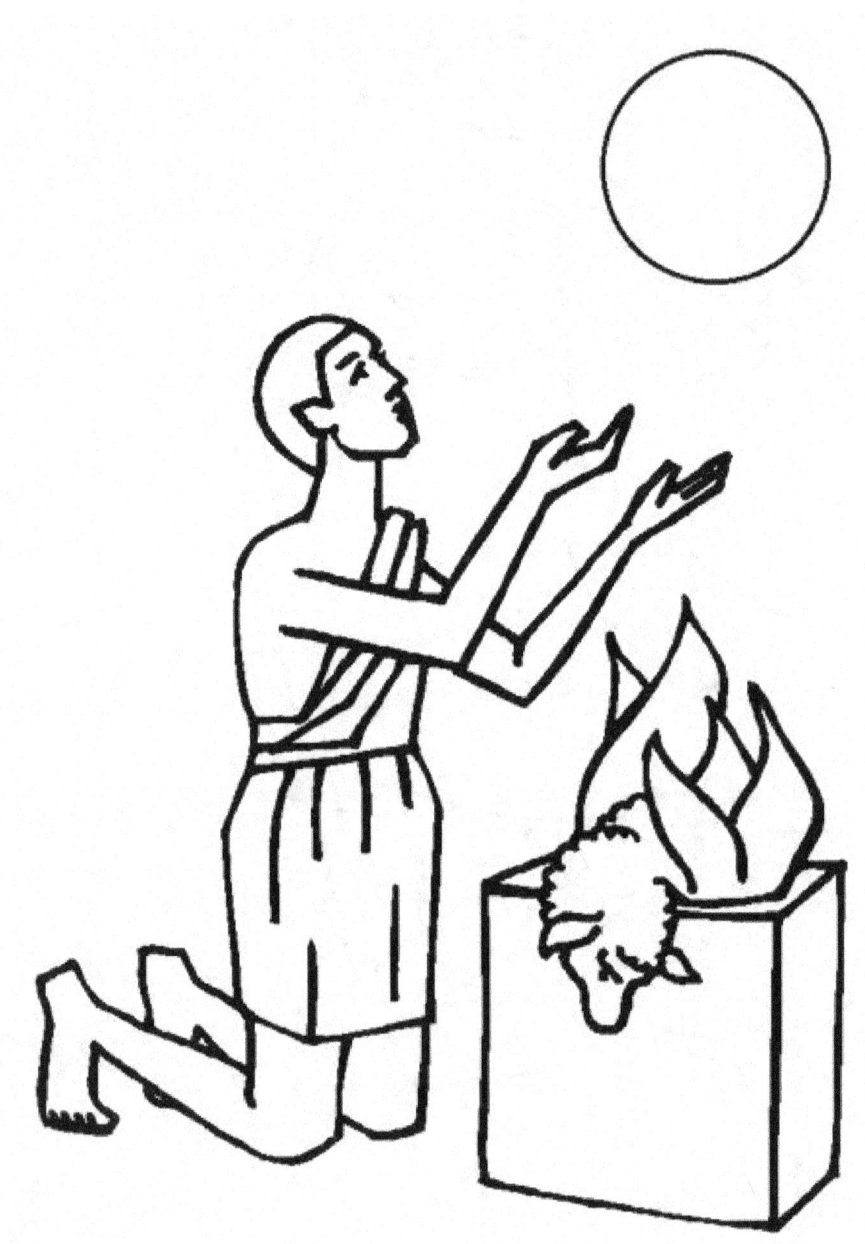

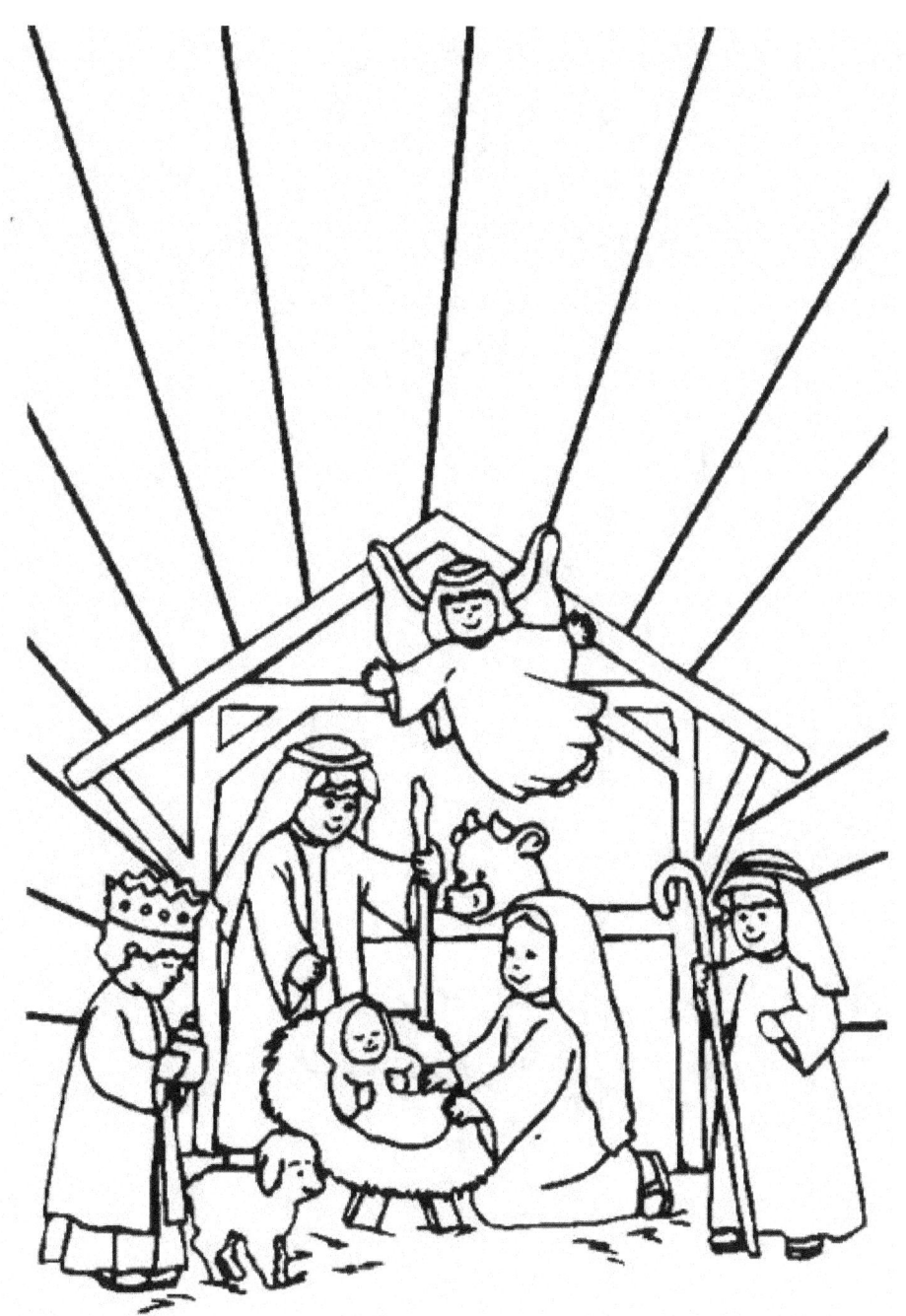

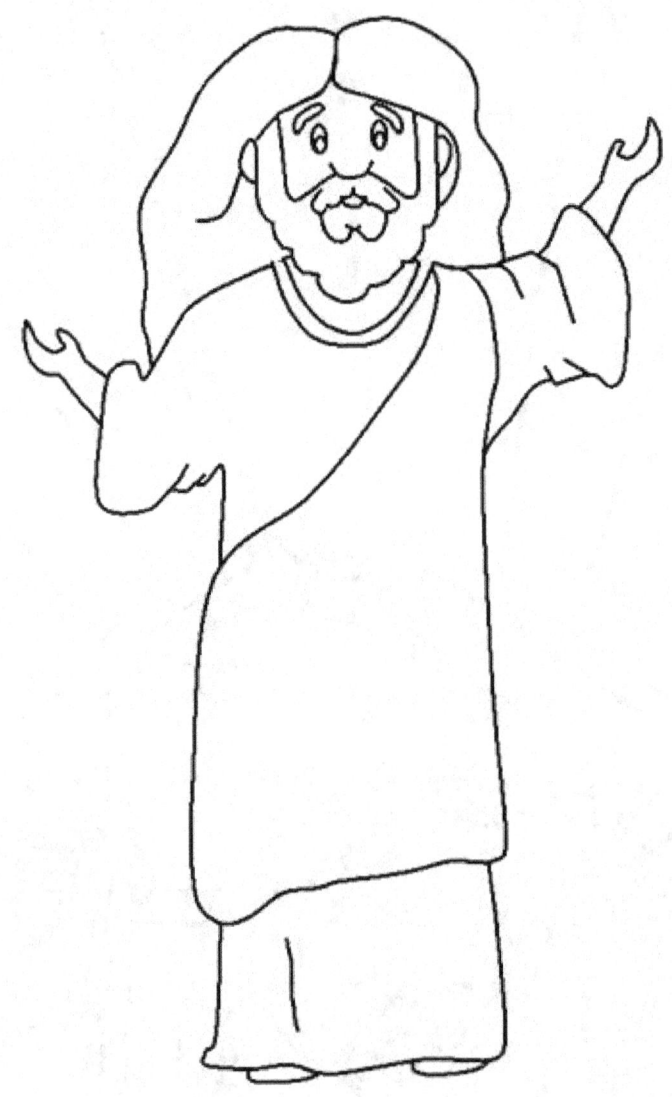

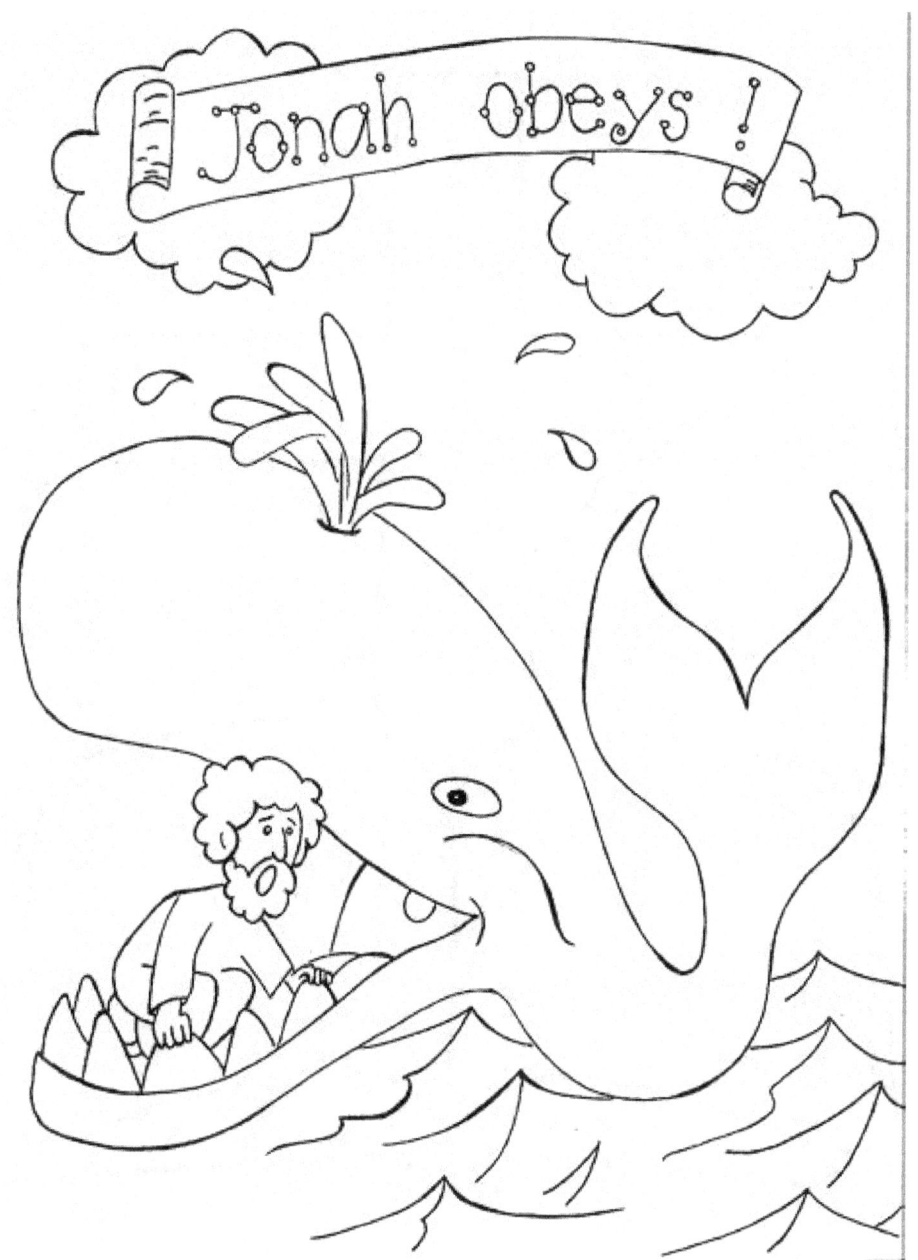

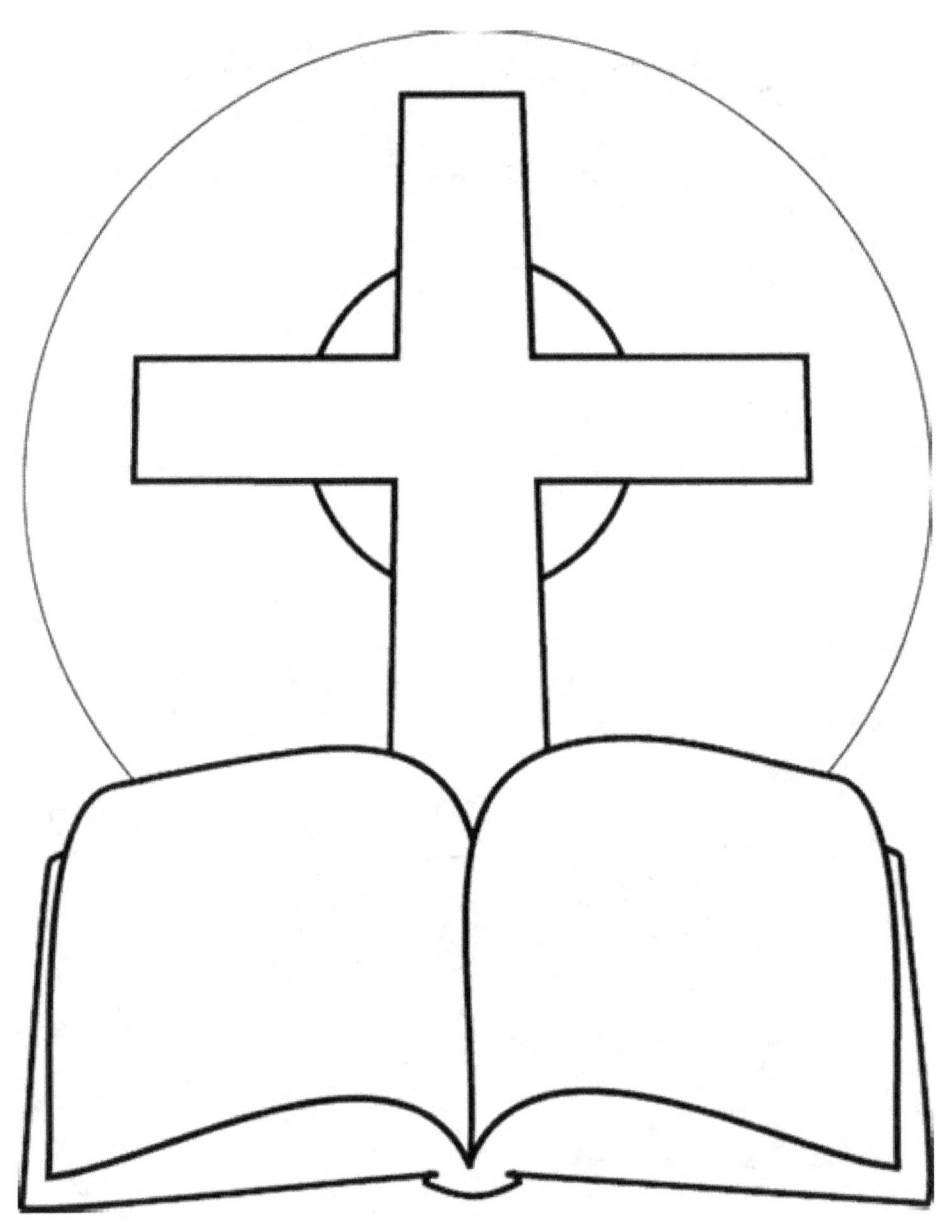

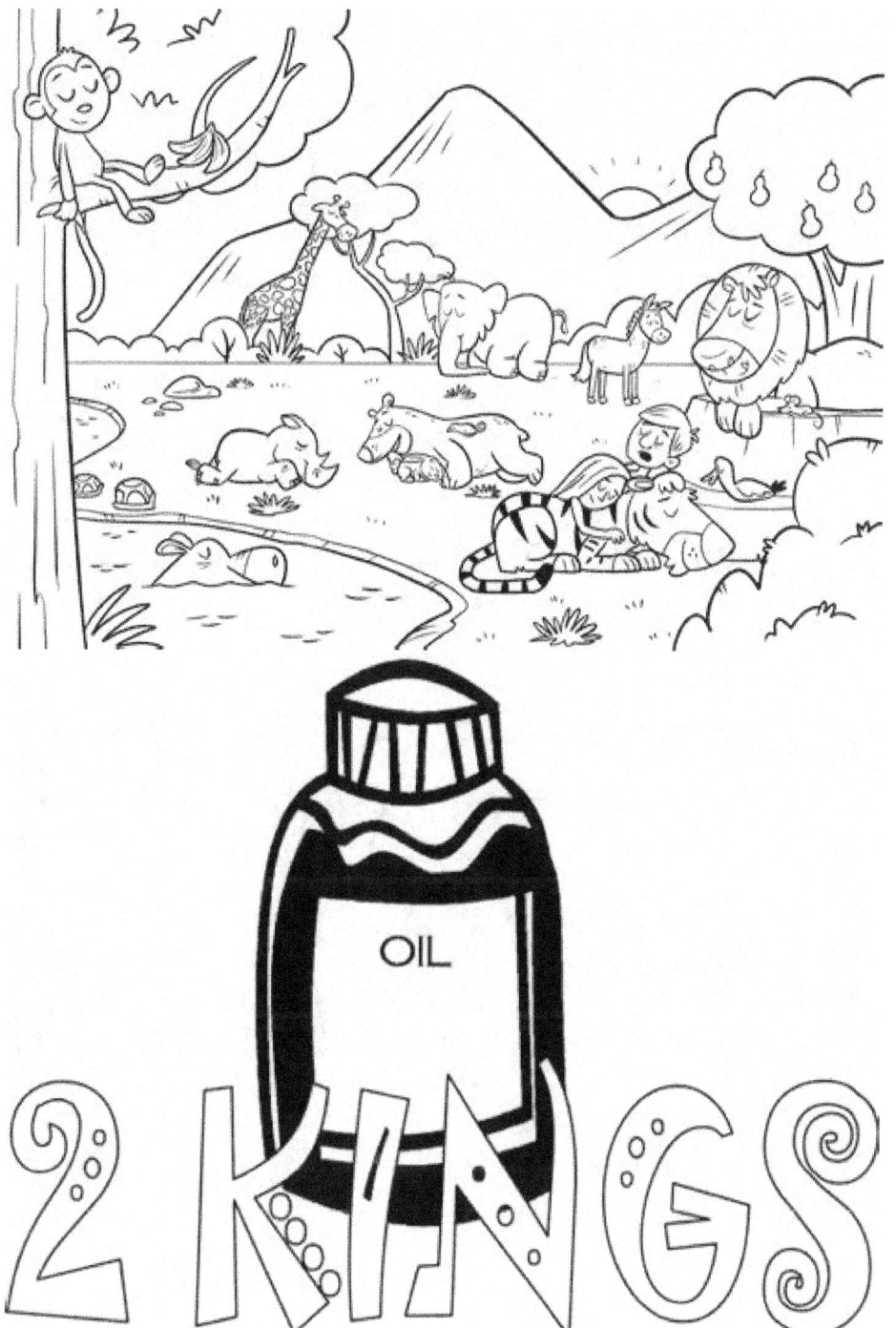

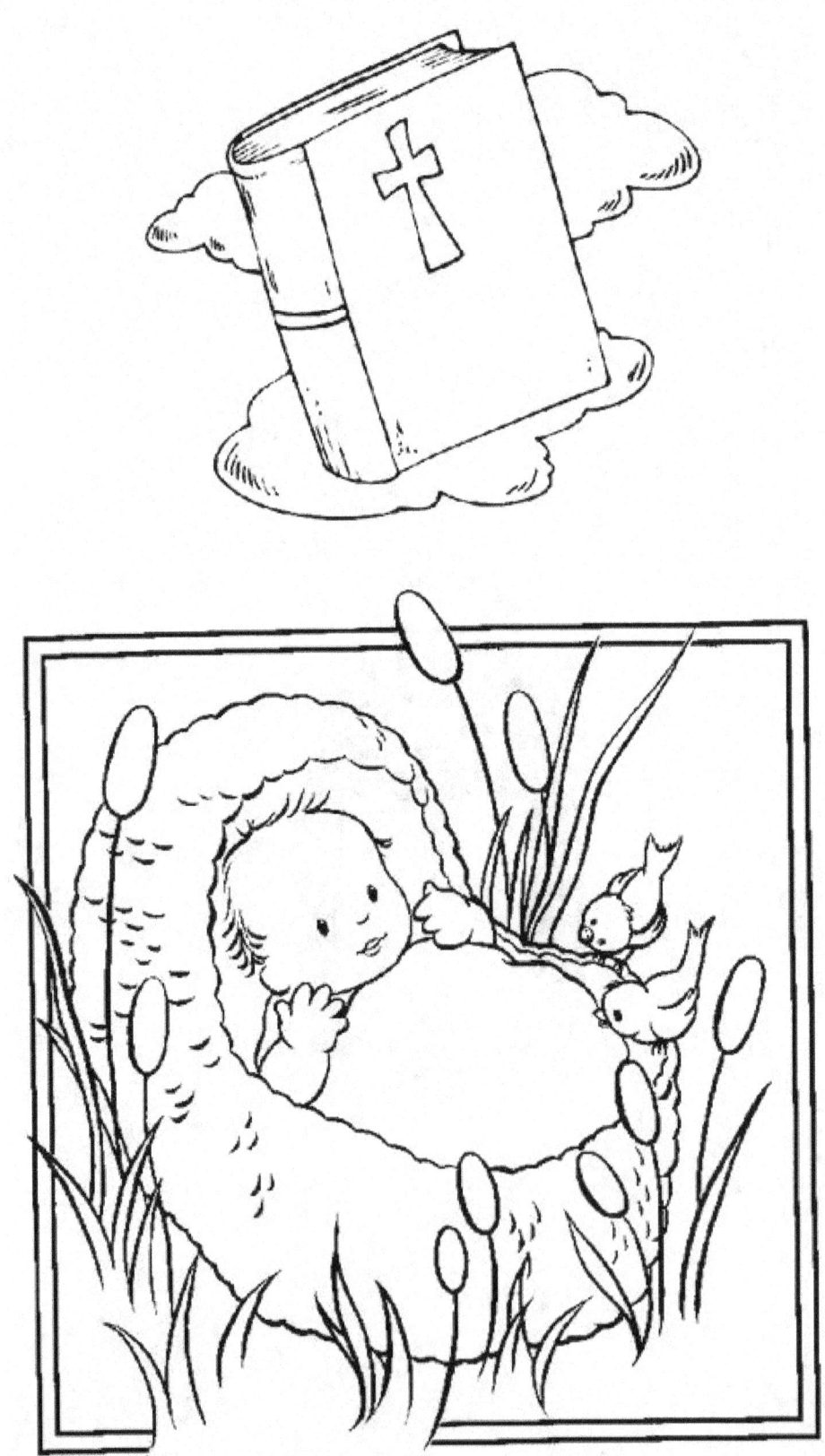

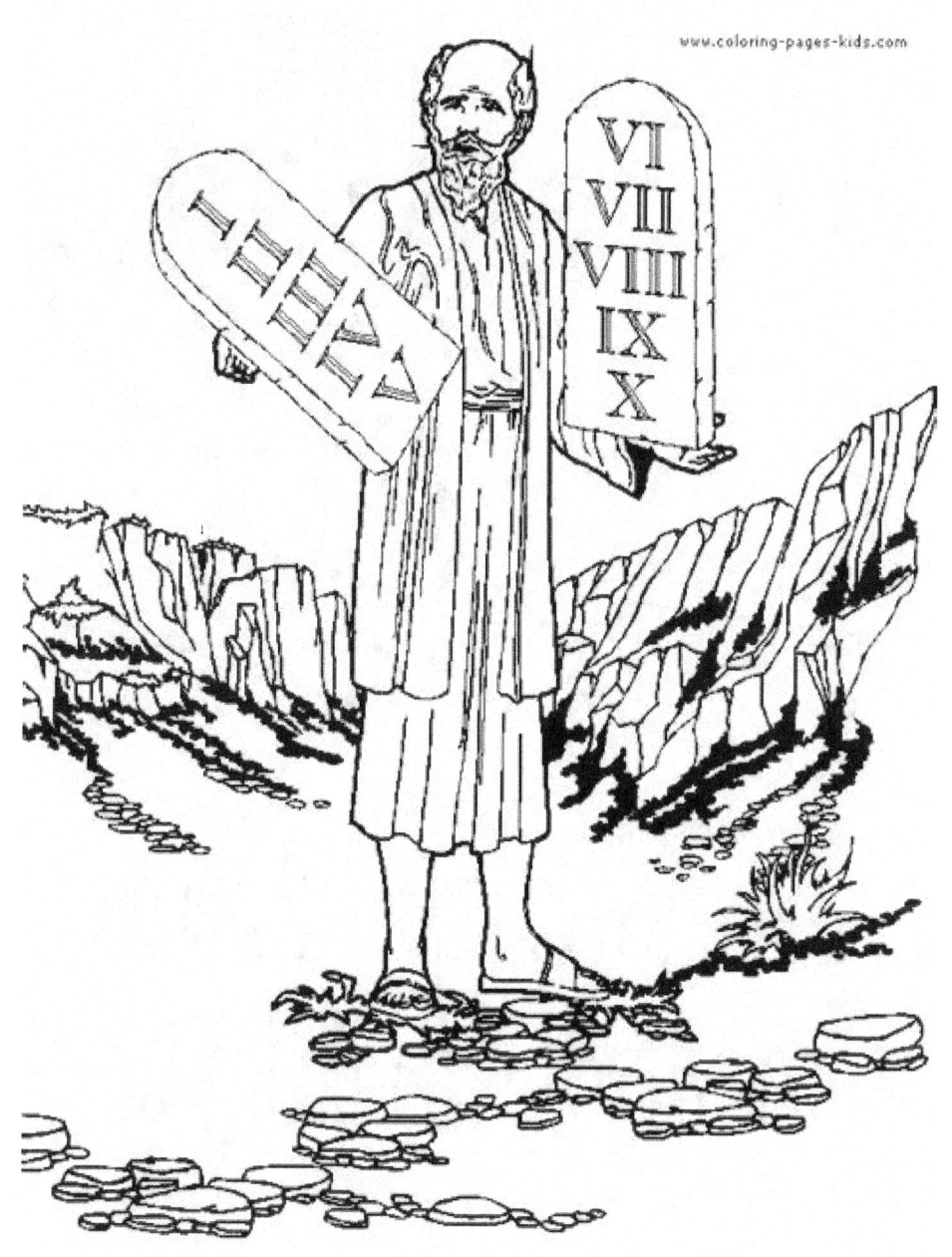

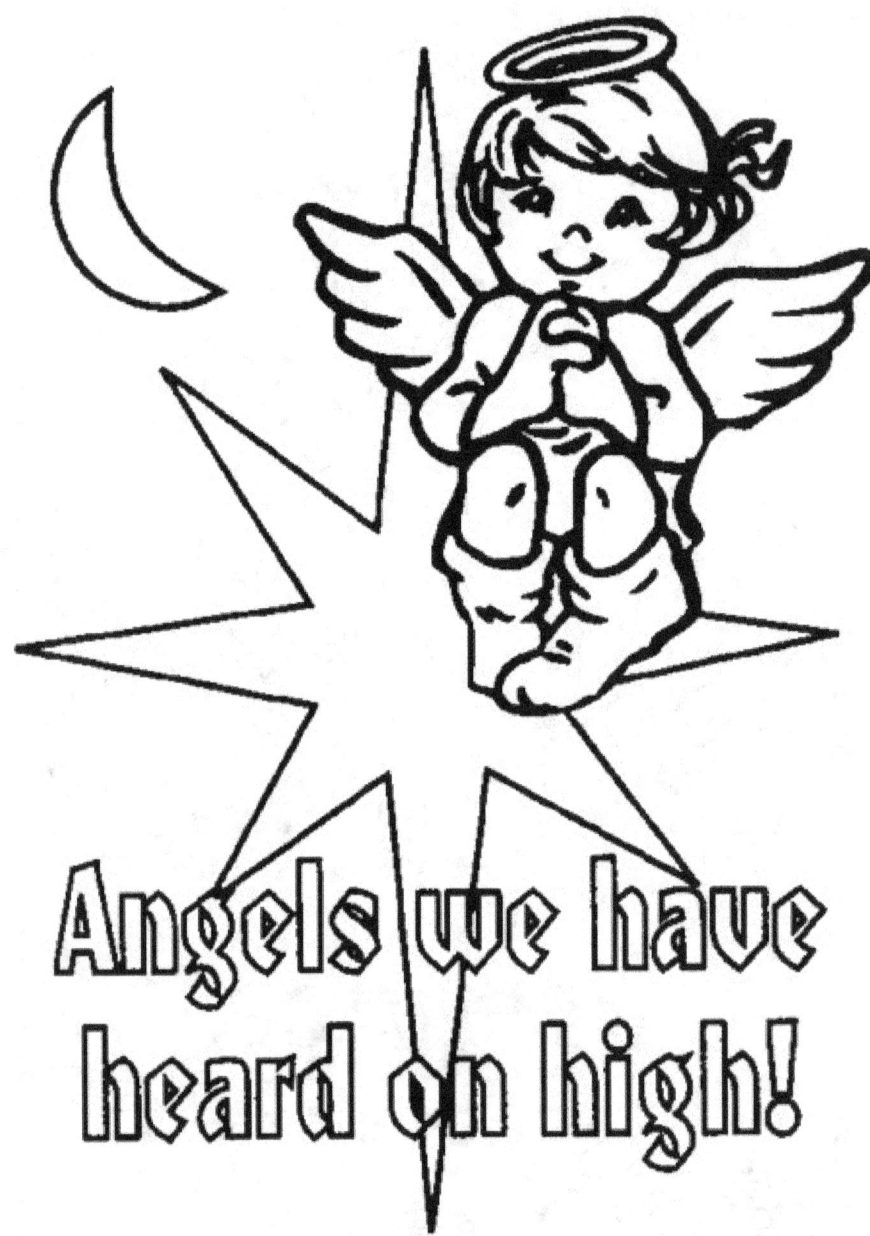

Angels we have
heard on high!

God saw all that He had made,
and it was very good.

Genesis 1:31

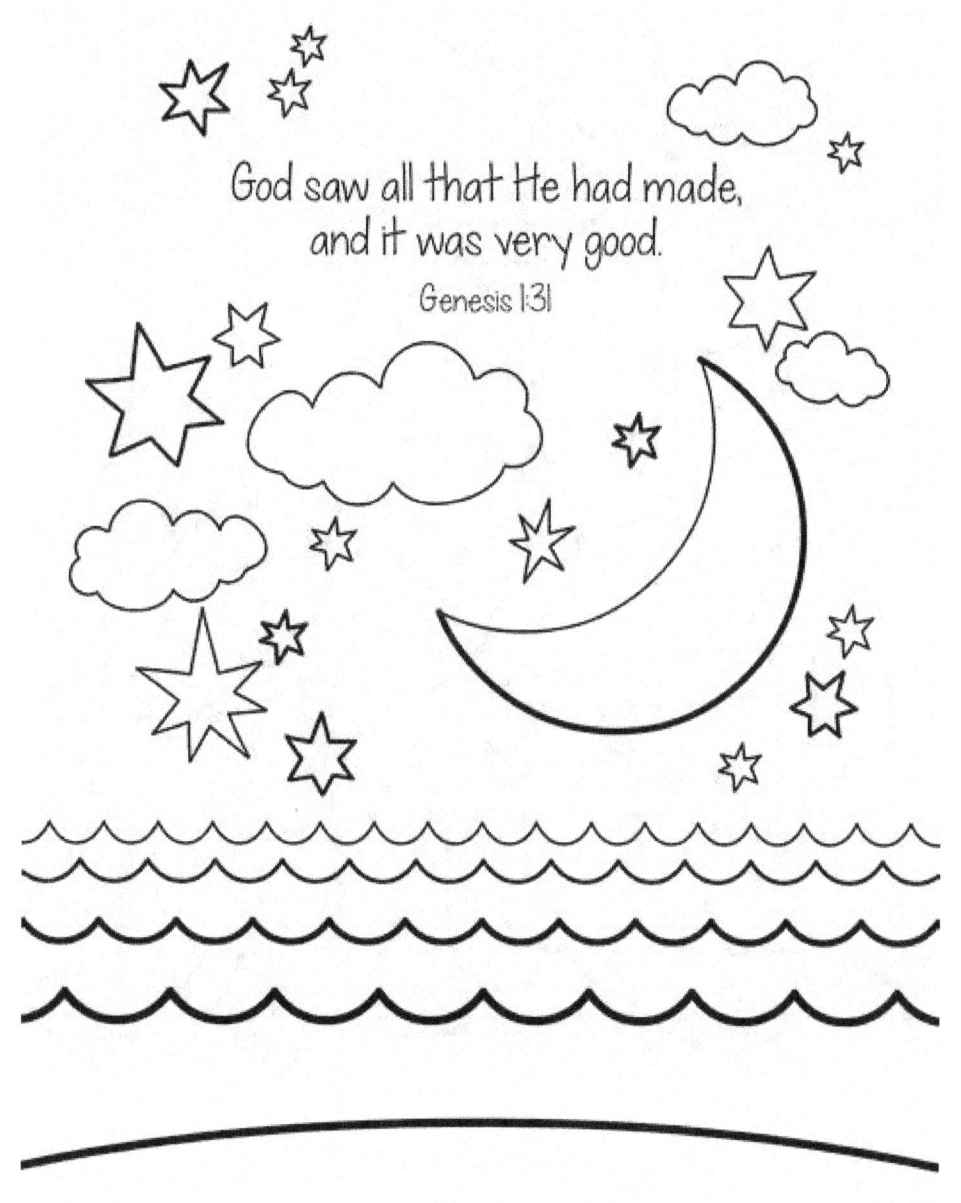

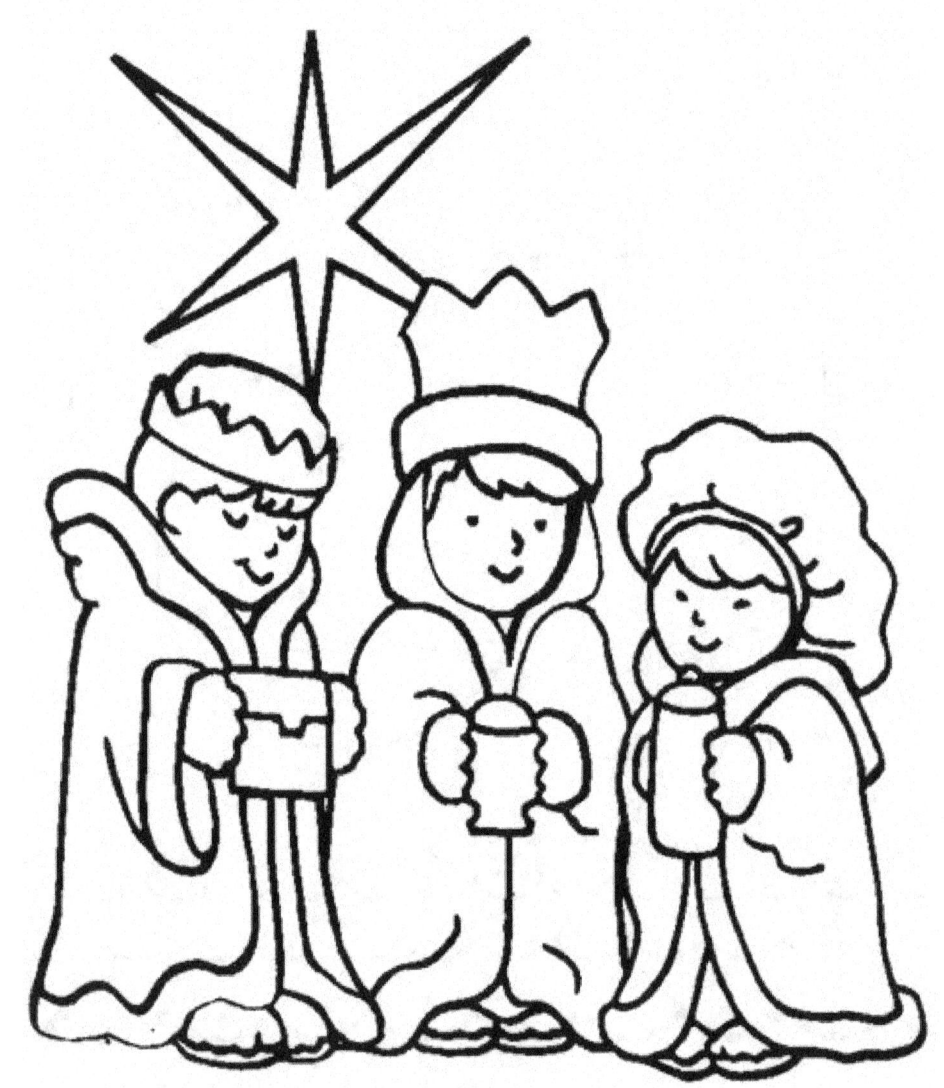

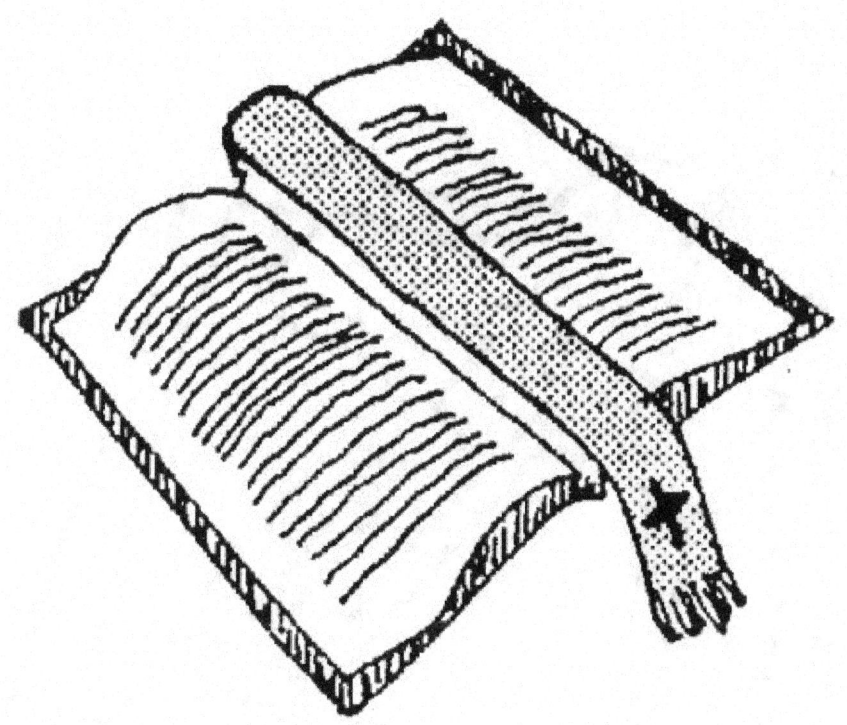

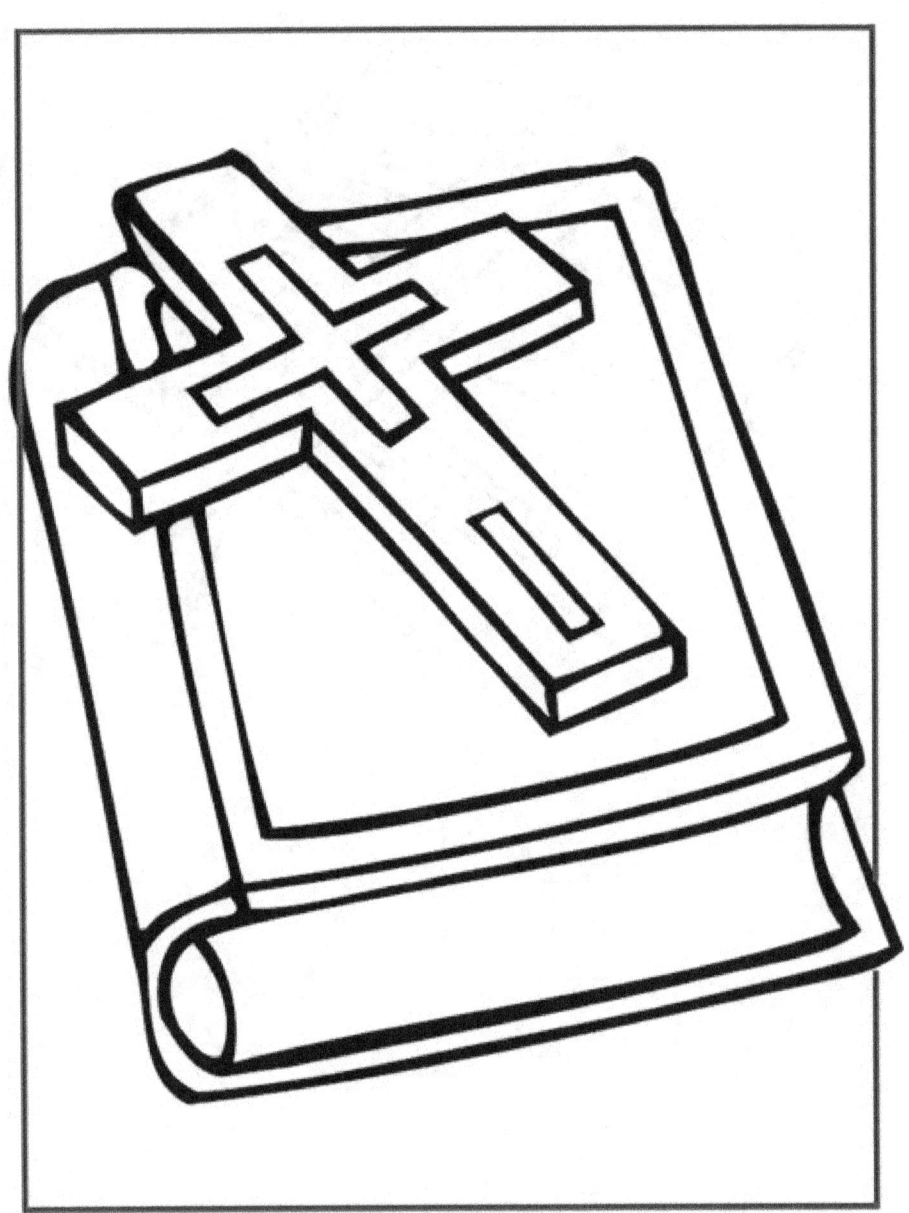

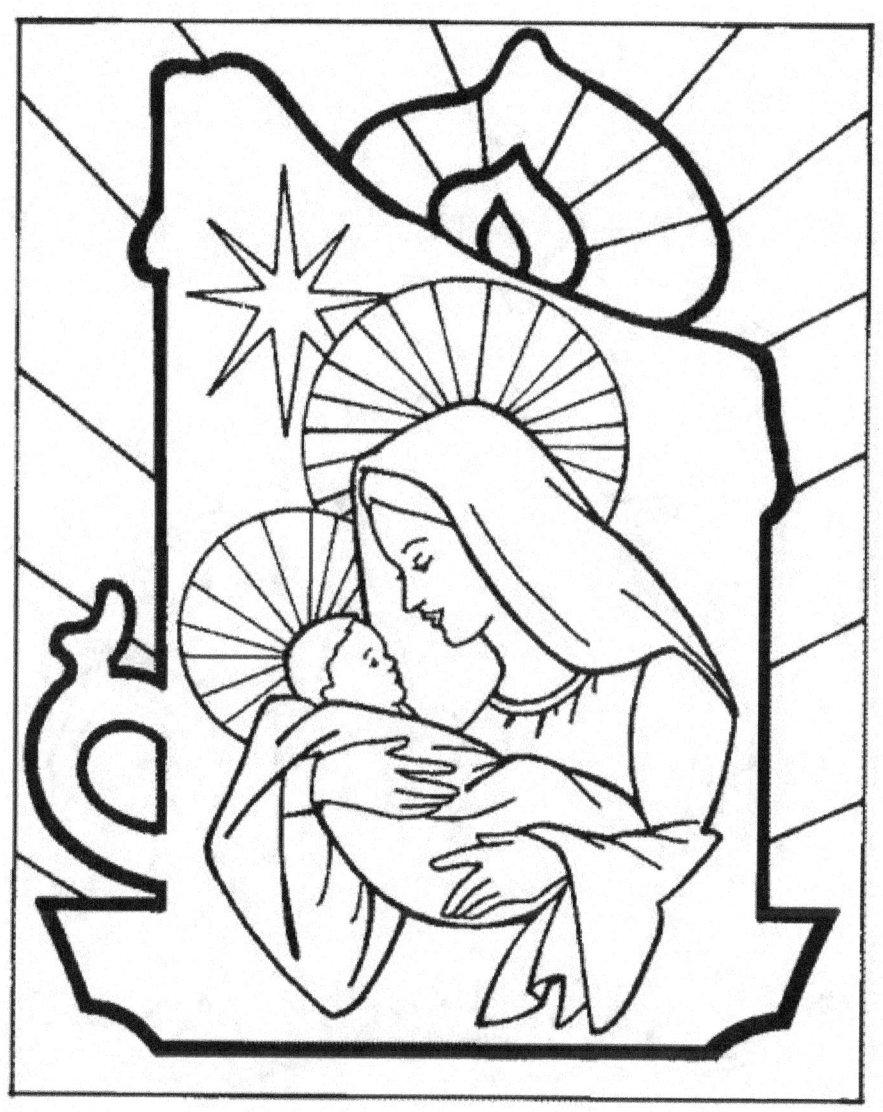

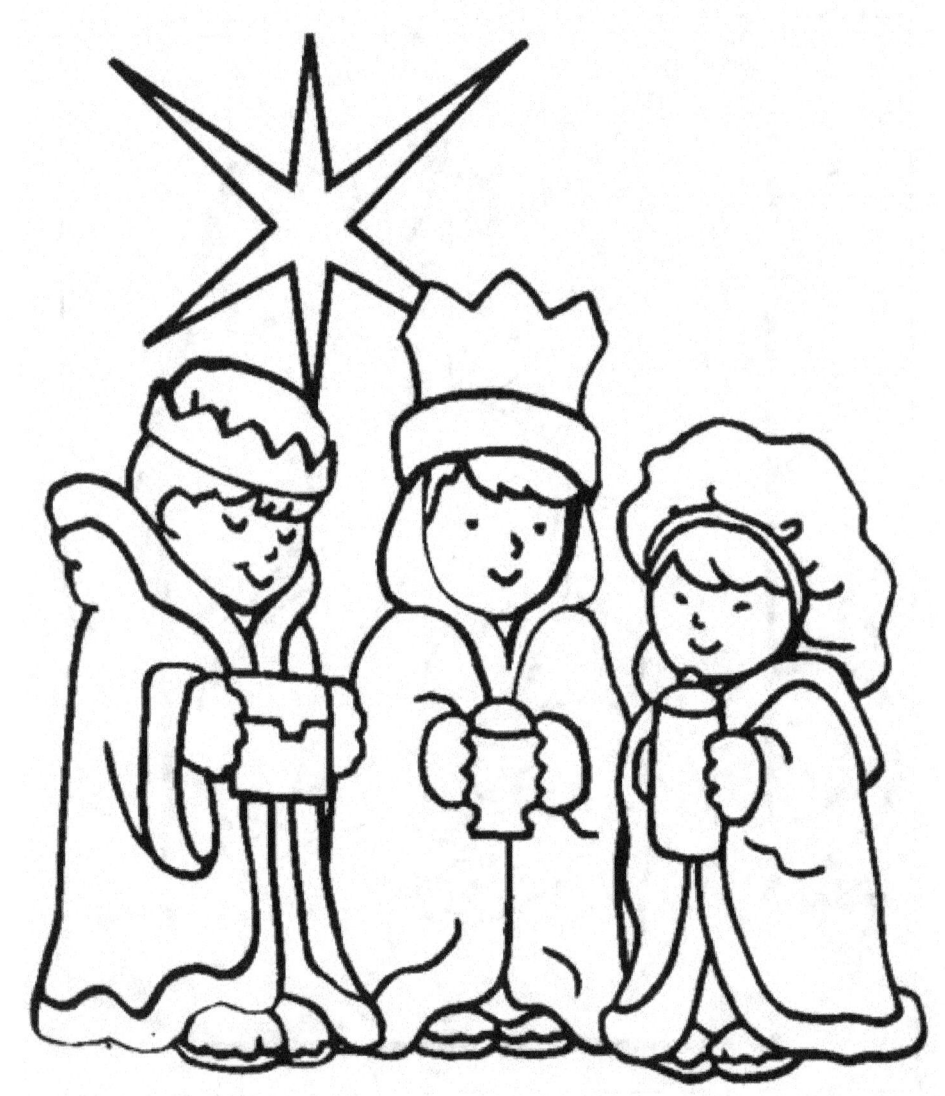

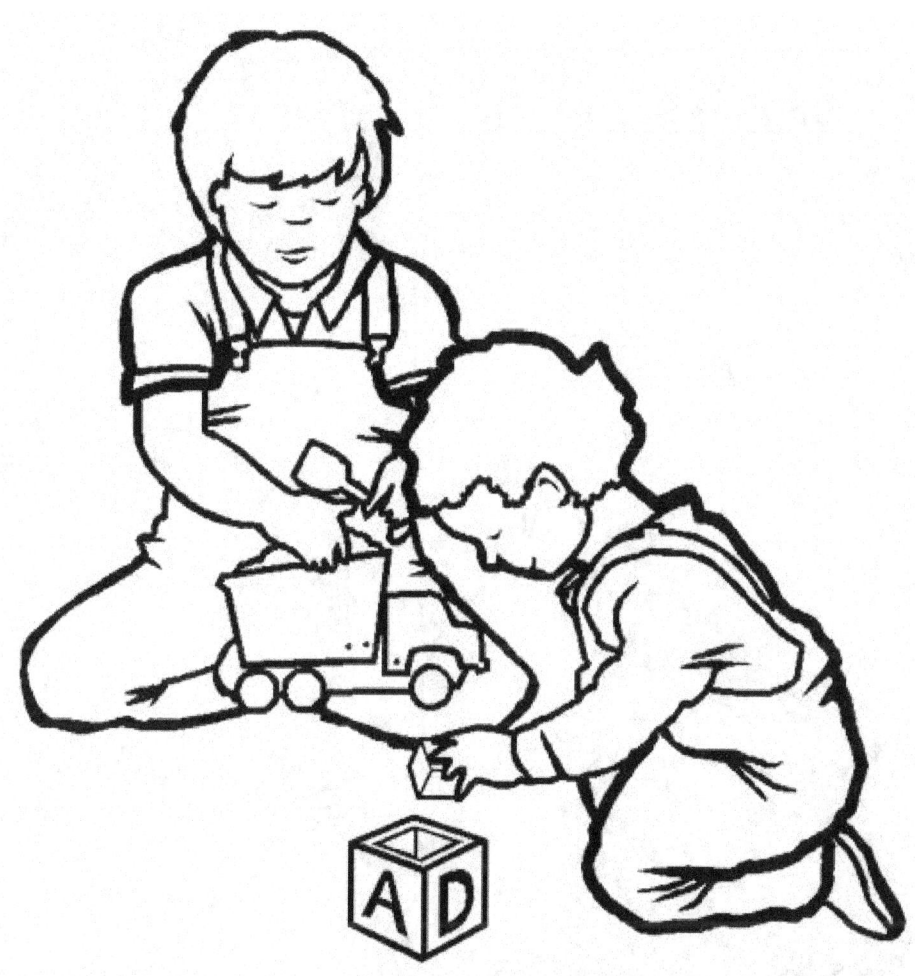

SHARE AND BE A FRIEND

I am my brother's keeper!

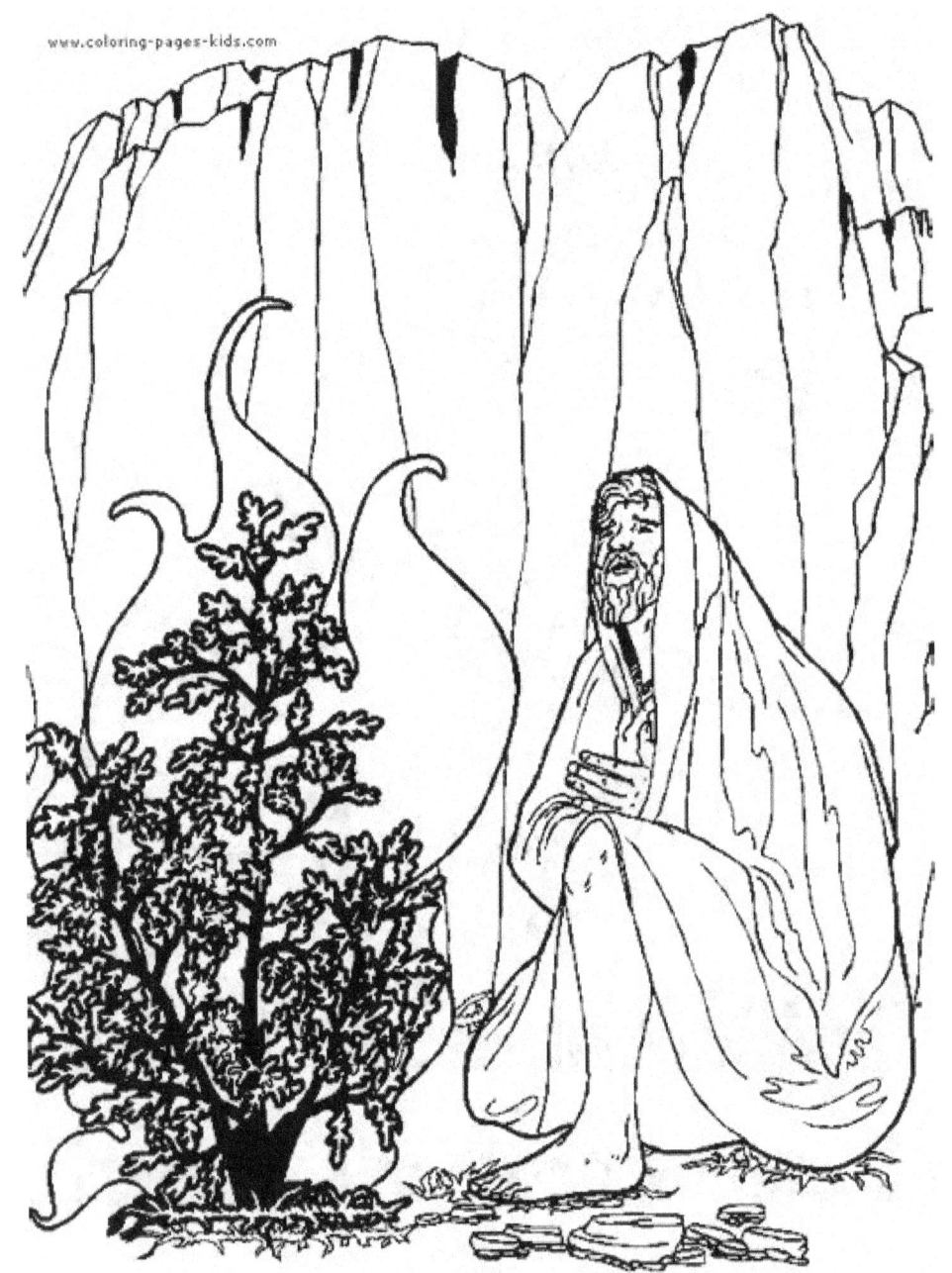

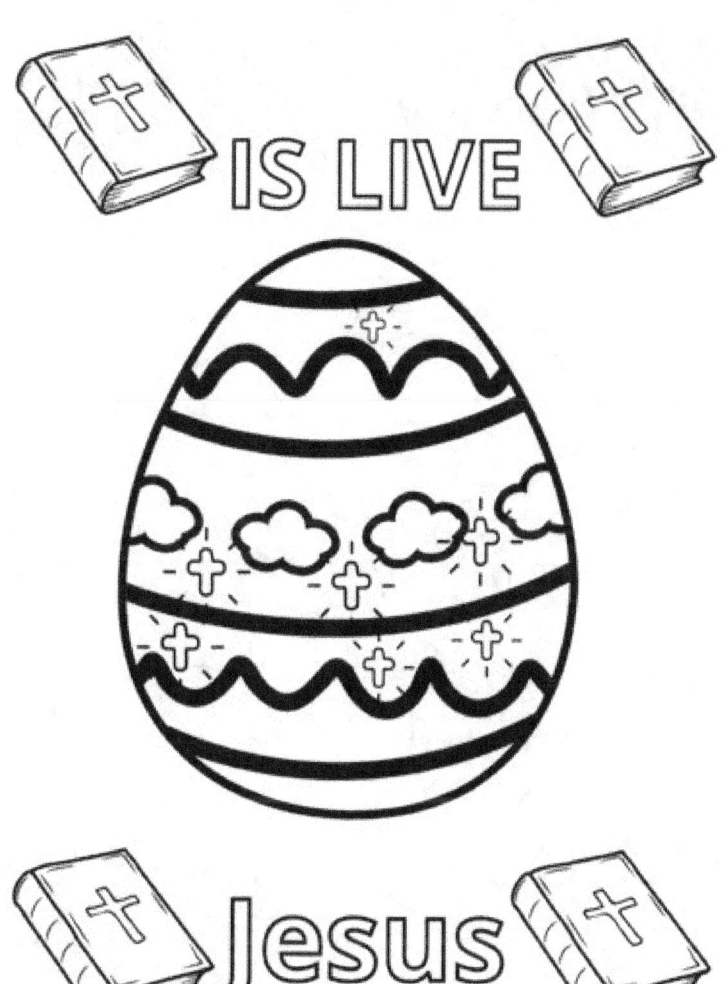

IS LIVE

Jesus

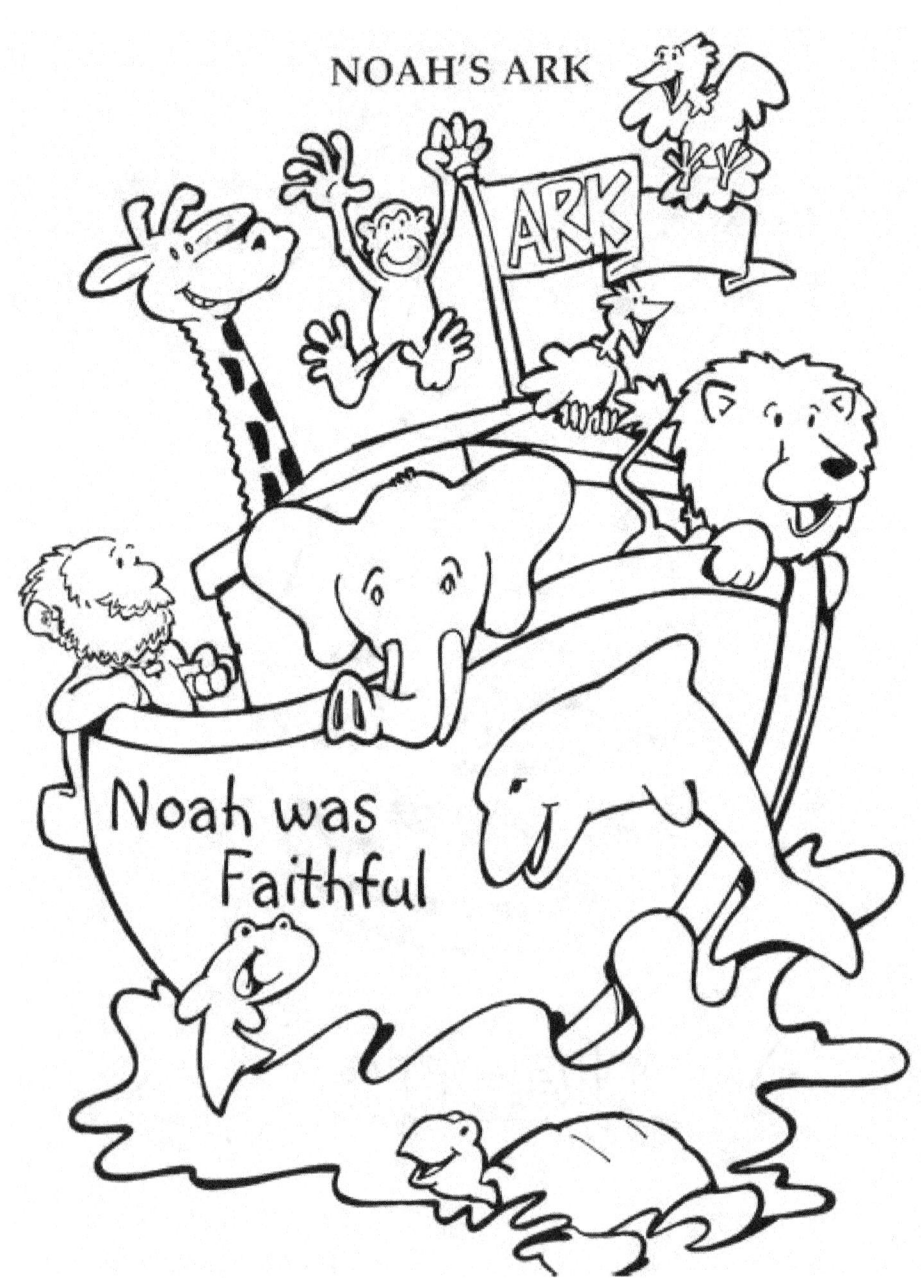

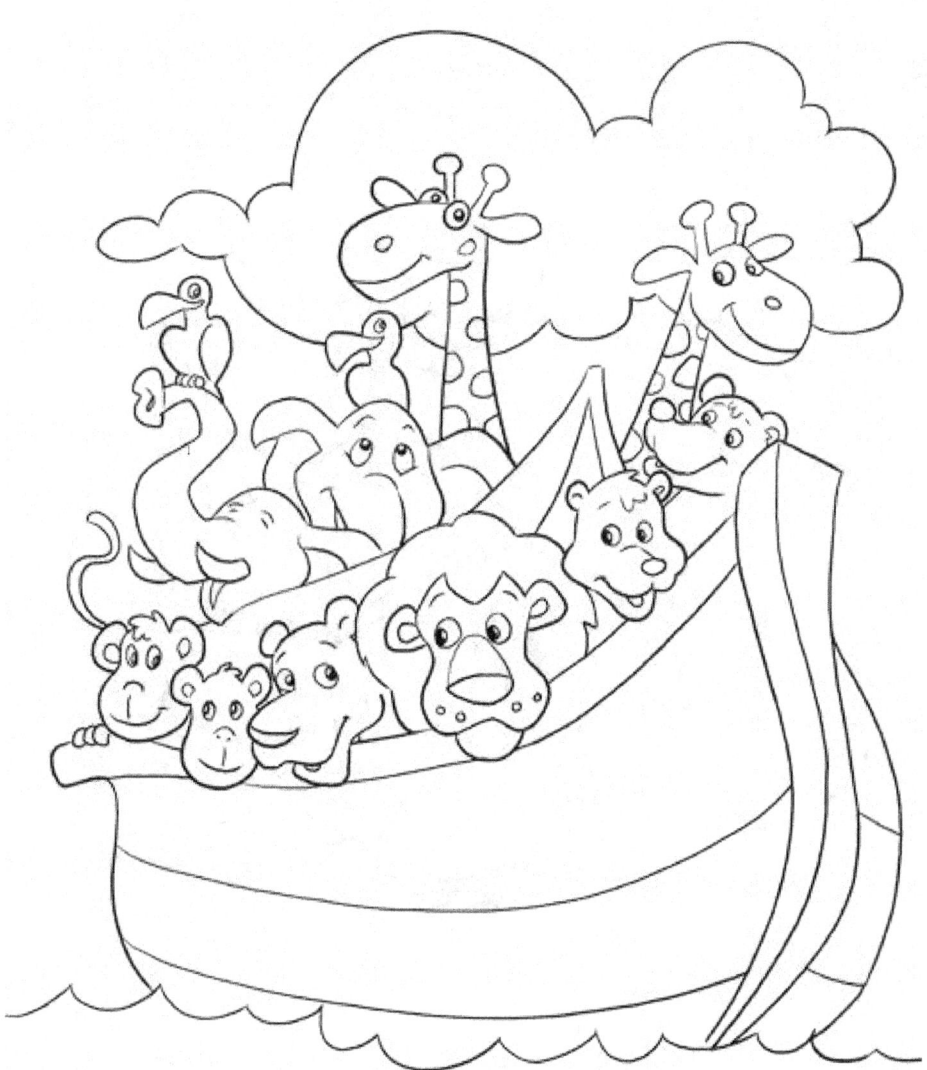

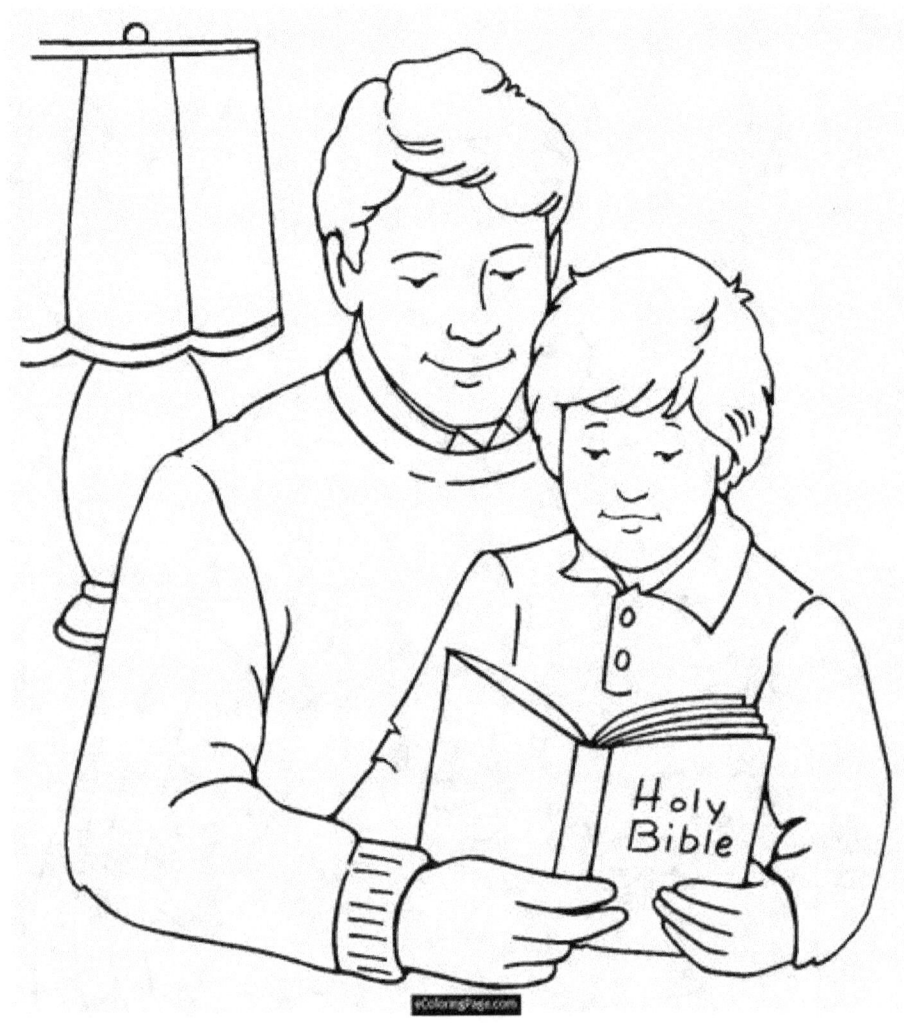